Handsome

stories of an awkward ~~girl~~ ~~boy~~ *human*

D0068249

Holly Lorka

She Writes Press, a BookSparks imprint
A Division of SparkPointStudio, LLC.

Published 2020
Printed in the United States of America

ISBN: 978-1-63152-783-8
ISBN: 978-1-63152-784-5
Library of Congress Control Number: 2020907228

For information, address:
She Writes Press
1569 Solano Ave #546
Berkeley, CA 94707

She Writes Press is a division of SparkPoint Studio, LLC.

This book is dedicated to my father,
whose sense of humor and stalwart belief in me
have made this life of mine possible.
I'm really sorry about some of these stories, Dad;
we don't ever have to talk about them.

And to George Michael, whose sweet ass keeps
showing up at important times in my life.

the captain
of some
ridiculous ship

*W*hen I was four years old, my friend Mikey told me that when he went downhill fast, like in a car, it made his pee-pee feel funny. I didn't understand what he meant until it happened to me. I was on a roller coaster with the Seven Dwarfs. All eight of us were sitting politely in our little cars, chugging up a steep incline with our hands on our safety bars, and when we descended rapidly while screaming and smiling, I got the greatest, most excited sparkly feeling in my pee-pee. It woke me up immediately. It was easily the best dream I'd had up to that point in my young life.

With some time and experimentation, I figured out how to make that feeling happen on purpose while I was awake. My mom had to take me to the doctor with frequent urinary tract infections because I was too young to understand the need to have clean hands when I had them stuck constantly down my pants. The doctor asked me, "Have you been touching yourself a lot down there?" Like I was going to admit to manually rubbing out thirty or forty sparkles every single day. I shook my head innocently and realized that I was either going to have to start washing my hands or figure out something else. So I made up humping, because I was smart.

I began rubbing around on my bed and bedroom floor with the fervor of someone on fire. My bedroom was upstairs, though, and in an effort to be more efficient, I discovered that the downstairs bathroom was also a fine place to hump. The floor was covered in blue shag carpet, and there was a lock on the door. The only problem was that because of the size of the bathroom, when I lay down on the floor to do it, my face ended up just behind the closed door. Unfortunately, this meant I could see everyone's shoes in the space under the door when they walked between the kitchen and the family room. Do you know how hard it is to keep your hump concentration on Shirley from *Laverne & Shirley* in the episode where she gets hit in the head, gets amnesia, thinks she's a stripper, and takes her clothes off at the Elks Lodge, when you have to watch your mom with her big toes scoot-clapping on by in her Dr. Scholl's?

But I would not be deterred. I humped soundlessly, all the while keenly aware of how long I was taking so as not to raise suspicion about what I was doing. When I was through, I'd make sure to fluff the shag back up. I was a careful little humper.

By some lucky fluke, I discovered that if I put something down between my legs while I rubbed around it felt even better. New and improved sparkles!

At first I used the My Size Barbie I won in the fourth-grade softball throw. I was pretty pissed when they gave it to me. I mean, what total jock wants a stupid My Size Barbie? The answer was: this horny little kid. Barbie was great, and the kind of pretty I liked, but I was lanky and I outgrew her quickly. Soon after, I started humping the hamburger pillow I sewed in sixth-grade home ec. It was just the right size and shape to fit where it needed to fit, so I got down with that pillow for years. I went on so many secret nighttime dates with that thing that I eventually rubbed one of the sesame seeds clean off the bun. Sure, it was a hamburger, but we had a good thing going.

Eventually, like when I was eighteen, I broke up with my hamburger, which by then had zero sesame seeds left on it, and I started exploring the possibility of making sparkles with other people, because that's what normal folks do. Things became awkward very quickly. I initially blamed it on the boners.

The first boner I met belonged to a cute bodybuilding guy. It was our second date. I was still living with my parents, and my dad was taking a nap in the bedroom next to mine. I brought my date into my room. We started making out and things got a little out of control, perhaps because our date was spent lifting weights at the gym. Next thing I knew, I felt his boner on my leg. As this was my first experience with a boner, it very quickly became the only thing in the room. I swear, it rose up and blocked out the sun. Everything became just *bonerbonerbonerboner*. My brain began shouting, *WHAT DO I DO WITH THIS BONER WITHOUT WAKING UP MY DAD?* The obvious answer, of course, was *defuse the boner*. Or, in other words: hand job.

I'd read about hand jobs. When I hadn't been busy humping shit on the floor of my bedroom, I read a lot. I tried to learn about having sex with other people from reading books because there was no Internet yet. In those books, the sex always seemed so amazing, hot, and perfect. I went on sleepovers where we stole my friend's mom's paperback novels like *Wifey* or *Endless Love*. As any curious kids would do, we turned immediately to the ends of chapters, where men's kisses set the skin of women's milky white breasts on fire and women handled the heavy throbbing of a man's member against her thigh with finesse and expertise. Their sparkles seemed easy and abundant.

Those books were obviously not written about a naive, eighteen-year-old honor roll shortstop whose only sexual experience up to that point had been with a doll and a hamburger.

I did a hand job with as much finesse and expertise as I knew how. Unfortunately for my date it was probably something close to yanking his dry penis off of his body while making sexy groaning noises and wondering why nothing actually throbbed. Luckily, he was a nineteen-year-old boy, so it only took him about three minutes to come. When he did, I closed my eyes, because no way did I want to see that. The problem was that he closed his eyes too and neither of us saw where his come went. It wasn't on my hand or on either of our pants. It had disappeared. I still lived with my parents. Sometimes they came into my room for stuff. WE HAD TO FIND THE COME BEFORE MY PARENTS DID.

Looking for come with someone you've only been on two dates with is a little awkward. My dad was still sleeping in the next room while we scrambled around in mine searching for it: on the bed, on the carpet, in my hair, on the ceiling (he convinced me it might be there). This was horrible and the least sexy thing I could imagine, aside from doing a hand job. We never found his magical disappearing come, which is how I always thought of it, until a girlfriend pointed out that maybe it was the worst hand job ever and probably it was so awful that he faked coming just so he could get out of there before I gave his dick an Indian sunburn. I was pretty sure no one was going to be flipping to the end of any chapters to read about this.

Which brings us to Boner Number Two. It belonged to Michael, a pretty fry cook who worked in the kitchen at my job. His eyes were very blue and I thought he was sweet. He asked me out for a drink after work. I assumed this meant he liked me and wanted to date me. I surely didn't think he was trying to get me into the back seat of his Pontiac to meet his boner, which he called his "Little Friend." But there's where I found myself. He kept pointing to his boner and saying, "Say hello to my Little Friend," as in "Suck my creepy dick." As I was incredibly naive and still thought we might hold hands at some point, I did my best to defuse the boner again. This time I made out with it, because I'm sure that's what Judy

Blume would've wanted me to do. Maybe it was that I had thought we were just going to talk, or maybe it was that I was in the back seat of a Pontiac with Scarface who smelled like French fries, but my first blow job was so much worse and more awkward than my first hand job. There was no come, magical or otherwise, and Michael never talked to me after that. It was Boners: 2, Holly: 0. Clearly, everything I'd read in those books wasn't helping me at all.

As boners weren't doing anything for my quest for sparkles, I eventually weaned myself off them and hoped that the awkwardness of sex would go away too. But it turns out that boners weren't the problem. *Sex* was actually the problem. Those sparkles could be elusive motherfuckers.

Shortly after I decided that boners weren't for me, I started having sex with girls. While my pants became much happier, there was still plenty of the awkward to be had. One night, I was sitting up in bed naked with a girl when she suddenly shimmied underneath me, pulled me up over her, and told me to sit on her face, because I obviously looked like a person who wants to sit on a chick's face???? (If I look like any part of a face-sitting bonanza, it's definitely NOT the sitter.) I was stunned and found myself holding onto my headboard, like the captain of some ridiculous ship, cautiously lowering myself down like I was about to dip into icy water. I reluctantly made it down onto her expectant mouth and realized I didn't know the first thing about face-sitting protocol. I'd never sat this close to someone's eyes before. What is the maximum weight load for a face? Was there supposed to be a safe word? How would I hear her if she were to say it? This was worse than boners. There were no sparkles here.

It was the same feeling as when I was scissored by a girl. She was very athletic. She maneuvered herself around and managed to slide a leg up under my back so that she could spread her legs and smear her parts all over my parts in that most ancient of Sapphic mating rituals. It was like having a women's studies class right there in my bedroom. I kept almost taking a foot in the face while she writhed around and eventually got off while Ani DiFranco wailed in the background. Why couldn't we just finger bang, rescue a Chihuahua together, and make some hummus, like normal lesbians? Things were much simpler when it was just me and my hamburger.

But I can't go back to simple. None of us can. We grow up and into a world beyond the Seven Dwarfs, Barbies, and humpy pillows that Judy Blume never bothered to tell us about, that E. L. James just flat-out lies about. It's a world where translating making sparkles by ourselves into making them with other people is awkward. No one tells us the truth about it, and that's not cool. Some horny kid's going to find and sneak the BDSM atrocity *Fifty Shades of Grey* under the covers at night with a flashlight and be fucked up forever, especially when they discover boners for real. We can't keep doing this to people. We need to stop being chicken shits and just tell the truth, so folks know how important it is to watch where the come lands.

This is a book of non-chicken-shit stories about awkward sex, great sex, imaginary sex, and being the wrong sex. It's about some normal stuff too, because even the best life can't be all about sex. Sometimes there are also things like school and jobs and banjos.

P.S. Don't let your kids actually read this.

Photo by: Michael Lorka Jr.

off by
just a little

remember Halloween when I was in kindergarten. I was dressed as a cowgirl, which was the closest my mother dared get to my request to be a cow*boy*. The grade school parade preparations found me sitting on the carpeted steps of the library in my little red cowgirl outfit trimmed with black fringe and completed by the white handles of my pistols. I wished I could wear that outfit forever, except with pants instead of a skirt. I wished I could eat campfire beans and sleep on the ground instead of the bed I shared with my sister, wished my father drove a palomino horse instead of a Buick, wished I could worry about the sunrise and sunset instead of whether or not I would pee my pants that day. I wished I were a cowboy out in the desert—tired, dirty, and lean—so I could be alone and not worry about what I was or was not. I would ride out on the range and hear only the crickets and coyotes, my belly full of beans, grit in my teeth, the fringe hanging from my arms rolling in waves with the creosote breezes.

But instead I was in the library in a skirt. I was not a cowboy, I was not a boy at all, and I would probably pee my pants again that day. Goddammit, Mom. Goddammit, life.

the truth about cookies

*T*he loss of your innocence always comes as a surprise, I think. I doubt anyone wakes up and thinks, *Today's the day that something tender and beautiful, something swathed in Pixy Stix sugar and copper penny shine, will be ripped away from me like a scab.* There is no warning. For me, it happened on a fall night in 1993. I had no hints of the events to come, unless we count too many Zimas and songs from the new Wynonna Judd album as the ample omens they were.

In 1993 I came out as a lesbian. Up to that point, I'd had sex with numerous men, and it was mostly okay: a bump-and-grind hundred-meter dash where the only thing I was concerned with was crossing the orgasm finish line as fast as possible. The sex was always at least cordial. They had too much body hair, and my imaginary dick kept getting in the way, but generally it was nice, despite the messiness. Really, any would-be lesbian/straight man trapped in a woman's body who's ever walked to the bathroom with come running down her leg without being displeased with sex has had it pretty good.

Though I didn't really want to have sex with men. What I really wanted was to have sex with girls. I'd fantasized about it for nearly my entire life. In 1993 I finally did something about it. At the age of twenty-three, I dumped my fiancée, cut off my legendary perm, and sauntered on over to Homoville.

I remember sitting at my desk and writing in my journal after I came out about how wonderful my life was now going to be—about how women are so lovely and sweet and kind. I was sure that from then on, my life would smell like fresh-baked cookies and that tiny bluebirds would bring me my robe in the morning while the Indigo Girls serenaded me. It would be like an all-girl Eden, but with Bud Light longnecks growing on the trees instead of apples. There would be no more come running down my leg, ever.

When I became a regular at the gay bar, the bartenders there gave me a nickname. They called me "The Ivory Girl." I was shy and polite, I looked young and always showed up all scrubbed and shiny with my shirt tucked in and buttoned up to the collar because I believed that even if you have to be a gay, you can be a clean and nicely dressed gay. My nights at the bar were generally uneventful. I was nervous, and all I could muster were brief conversations with women that I didn't want to know. Mostly, I sat at the bar, drank a few beers, and kept to myself. It seemed being gay was kind of like being at the airport, except with less sex.

Then I met Jaime. She was my age, was cute, sweet, and funny. She bought me a drink and let me kiss her in the parking lot that night. We, both so very shy, barely touched each other except at the mouth, which was enough to melt us down to the concrete under our feet. Sweet Jesus, that kiss was better than any orgasm I'd ever had with a man. It was better than any fantasy I'd had about Stefanie Powers. It was when I discovered that my mouth was connected to my pants in ways I had never before imagined.

The next time I saw her we went to her place and had sex. Actually, I dropped her off at her place and drove away to park around the corner and wait because she lived in an apartment attached to her parents' house. They had no idea she liked girls, and I didn't look like a handsome young man yet. I had to wait in my car for an hour, then sneak under their front window around to the back of the house to rap softly on her glass-paned French door.

She let me in and we went to her room. I remember that we were listening to George Michael and trying to be quiet and it was all very sweet and very hot and maybe a little clumsy because we were both so new at gay. We spent such a long time together, exploring, moving against each other, listening and singing to "Father Figure." It lasted years or glorious weeks or just a few hours, I wasn't sure. That night was like watching a beautiful sunset that lasted forever. I left in the whisper of 4 a.m. to crawl back under the front window and around the corner to my car and drove away feeling light and buzzy-buzzy on what had happened.

We saw each other for a few months. She was a professional tennis player and out of town much of the time, so she'd send me affectionate letters from England or Australia. If she was in town, we'd meet at the bar and then we'd go back to her house and I'd park around the corner again to crawl under the front window. The classic romance story. I simply adored her, but her sponsors began to question her sexuality. Back in 1993, large sports companies weren't keen on sponsoring a lesbian. Jaime had to cut off anything that might look suspicious, which included our budding romance.

It hurt, but I certainly couldn't blame her. Playing tennis was her dream. Mine was to have more sex with women and maybe even to fall in love. I still believed in the bluebirds and the cookies, and, although I was sad, I believed I'd get to have those things with someone soon. So I went back to the gay bar to find them, because everyone knows the gay bar is where cookies and bluebirds live.

It was a Sunday night, and there weren't many people there. I was heartbroken and blue, the beer was flat, and I remember thinking I should just go home. Then someone sat down beside me.

She was older than me, easily in her forties to my twenties. She was attractive and well dressed, and looked like she also believed in being a clean gay. She said hello and introduced herself. I knew immediately that she was going to try to pick me up. I could smell it like I could smell her New West perfume, and I was interested in letting anything improve my situation.

I normally drank beer, but she bought me a Zima. We chatted. When we got to a lull in what would have been normal conversation, she upped the game by lifting an eyebrow to mention how magnificent she was. She owned a business, blah blah . . . another Zima. She had a nice house downtown, blah blah . . . another Zima. She drove a fast car, blah blah . . . another Zima. I was getting quite drunk. Or, more specifically, she was getting me quite drunk on purpose. At some point, perhaps when we heard Wynonna for the second time, I started to feel uncomfortable. The little red warning light that we all have started its dull glow in the back of my head. But it was up in my head, so very far away from my pants, where I desperately wanted to feel the hot buzz of sex with a woman again. So, when she offered to take me in her amazing car to her amazing house, I slurred, "Sure."

I don't remember what kind of car she drove, but I bet it was red. I do remember her house. It was mid-century modern, clean. All of its expensive surfaces were very shiny. She poured me a drink, took me by the hand, and led me back into her bedroom.

It was quiet except for the low hum of an enormous saltwater aquarium. I thought she might put some music on, but instead she ushered me directly to her bed. There was immediate kissing, which led to groping and to humping. The red warning light was glowing pretty brightly by now. I wasn't enjoying myself as much as I thought I would, thanks to twenty-three Zimas, a glass of whiskey, and a complete lapse in judgment. But I forged on, bolstered by the promise of cookies and bluebirds, of camping and poetry and women's music festivals and all the things that were going to make sleeping with women so much lovelier than sleeping with men.

I took her clothes off and I was lying on top of her, doing all the things I thought I should do, going slowly as I had with Jaime. Minutes in, while I was still navigating her skin with a gentle mouth, before I even moved my hand anywhere near her end zone, she gave me a stern command: "Put two fingers inside of me." Initially, it stopped me, this command. Though I was a fairly new lesbian and hadn't gotten that far into the instruction manual yet, I understood that two fingers is a fairly standard move. I'd have gotten there soon enough. I guessed she was just so obviously turned on by my awesome initial moves that she couldn't wait. So, though there was nothing sweet about how this was happening, I put two fingers into her.

I began to get seriously turned on, because that's what happens when I find my way into a vagina. I was breathing heavily, sweating, watching her through my dilated pupils, feeling that wonderful heavy, beating warmth in my own pants. I was thoroughly enjoying myself when she spoke again.

"Put three fingers inside of me."

For the record, two was all I'd ever done. But this woman was older. Maybe when you get older you need three. I put my best three into her and continued like a champ. Though my rookie pitching arm was getting tired, my pants were still on fire with delight. She spoke a third time.

"Put another finger into me," she commanded.

Um. Wait, now . . .

Even while drunk I knew that made four and four is too many. Four is a hand. Four is something you have a conversation about first, isn't it? Four was a chapter I hadn't expected to find in the manual. Four is when my pants went cold and the red light in my head went on so brightly that it made my scalp burn. I was being commanded, sternly, to do something that made me uncomfortable, something

I didn't really want to do, and something that didn't seem lovely to me at all. But I scrunched my fingers tightly together and four is what I did, because I agreed to all of this, didn't I? I let her buy me drinks, I came here in her car, and I got into her bed. Now I had my hand inside of her, and I hoped it would all be over soon because I was getting pretty creeped out. Also, because my arm was about to fall off.

That's when she said it.

"Put your fist into me." She wasn't looking at me when she said it. In fact, I don't think she looked at me at all that night. It's like I wasn't even there. We could have been strangers standing at a bus stop, where I was incidentally shaking hands with her vagina. I was an arm, a hand, a fist that she was commanding, that she somehow earned the right to command. My red light was now setting the room on fire. *SAVE ME, GEORGE MICHAEL*, it screamed. I wanted to take my hand and run away, to Jaime's house, to my parents' house, to kindergarten or somewhere else nice and sweet. But I didn't run. I was a deer caught in the headlights. A deer that was balling its right hand into the smallest fist imaginable. When I squeezed my five fingers into the stretching, sloppy warmth of her, surprised that they fit, I felt myself leave my body a little bit. I looked at me and what I was doing—reluctantly punching this stranger in the vagina while she wouldn't even look at me—and realized that the cookies and bluebirds were just some stupid shit I'd made up about sleeping with women. I'd fucked much nicer men than this woman. There may be more of these women out there. I should be more careful, and I should never go home with someone I don't know, at least not in her car, even if it's very fast and probably red.

When my arm gave out, when there was nothing more to put inside of her, when she was finished, I pushed myself off and put my shoes on while she got dressed. We walked outside and got into her car. After she started the engine, she looked directly at me and she said one last thing.

She said, "Do you want to go to Whataburger?"

Did I want to go to Whataburger? After that? After she gobbled up every bit of my tender innocence with her hungry vagina? I thought about what had happened that night, about what I'd lost and the knowledge I'd gained. For the second time that night, I slurred, "Sure." If I couldn't have cookies, at least I could have a goddamned Whataburger.

isn't it good

*S*aturday was the best day. That was the day my dad would mow the lawn, which meant I could help him mow the lawn. By help, I mean I could go get him a beer when he asked for one. By get him a beer, I mean I could open it and drink some of it before I gave it to him. That's what I mean. Every time I brought him a beer, he'd hold the can up and shake it a little before grinning and saying, "This one feels a little light, Holly." But this story isn't about how I started drinking beer when I was seven. This story is about my dad.

Every Saturday afternoon when I was seven or eight or nine, my dad went out and cut the grass. When he was done, he'd wrangle up the three of us kids and plop us down in the family room with our box of toys. He'd put a couple of his prized Beatles tapes in the Zenith dual-cassette stereo system and lie on the couch to take a nap while the Beatles wound from one reel to the next and we played around him.

My house wasn't safe. It looked fine, but it was full of poisonous snakes, booby traps, and witch hunts. Of crocodiles and surprise pools of quicksand. It was full of my mom, with her anger and harshness and family meetings at two in the morning that would leave us all terrified and skittery. My house was swollen with fear of her.

My mom didn't want to be a mom. It was clear to all of us that she longed for some other life, one that was much more glamorous. I guess it was difficult accepting her reality as the mother of three young kids living in Nebraska with a man who drove a Buick. When she met my dad, he drove a red Chevy convertible. He liked to dance. He was charming and handsome and swept her off her feet with his fancy jitterbug moves. But that was a long time ago, and by the time I was seven he was a blue-collar machinist with dirty fingernails who drove a sedan and drank canned beer, and together they had us. This was not the stuff her childhood dreams were made of. This was not what she would have chosen for herself. And though it wasn't on purpose, she punished all of us for it, scolding and yelling and pointing her finger. She blamed us for how underwhelming her life had turned out.

But on Saturday my mom went to work, and we and our house could finally open our eyes and stop pretending to be invisible. We could breathe, loosen our shoulders, laugh, and maybe even throw toys and socks on the floor. She was gone and we were with my dad.

My dad didn't say much. When he did speak, he liked to drop silly lines that he'd gleaned from the TV and then crack up at himself. "I may not be good, but I'm slow," was what he said when he finished putting my new blue banana seat bike together or building us an ice-skating rink in the backyard. "That's all for now, there'll be a little more later," is what he said when he did something good, like swish a basket from the far edge of the driveway while we looked on with our tiny mouths hanging open. He was good-natured, calm and steady. He taught us the important things, like how to skip rocks, how to leg wrestle, how to open a beer. He gave us pocketknives, taught us how to whittle, and didn't freak out when we cut the shit out of ourselves. He never threatened to leave, never raised his voice, and never pulled us out of bed for a family meeting at two in the morning.

My dad was safe. He was our shark-proof cage, our home plate. He told us we were precious and made us feel as though we were.

Every Saturday my brother and sister and I got to hang out with my dad and feel okay and also listen to the Beatles. Every Saturday was a different mix of tapes, but we heard every album and song so many times that I had all of it memorized: all of the albums, all of the words. I'd always get excited when I heard "Drive My Car," because I knew that was the first song on *Rubber Soul*, and up next was "Norwegian Wood." That weird little song was my favorite.

"I once had a girl. Or should I say, she once had me." I was seven. Every single time it came on I stopped playing with my Adventure People and tried to absorb what I was hearing—that instrument that sounded like a guitar out of tune, those lyrics that were magical and a puzzle and sexy. Even at seven, I knew that song was sexy.

I listened and pictured John Lennon sitting on a white shag rug trying not to spill wine on it before being remanded to sleep in the bathtub while an obviously beautiful woman who could afford Norwegian furnishings—but no chairs—went off to slumber in her fluffy bed. That is what I saw in my head when that song played. I also could tell John Lennon was very disappointed at having to sleep in the bathtub and there was something intriguing about that, but I couldn't figure it out. I was seven! I was just barely figuring out beer—I had no idea about trying to get laid.

After his nap, after we'd heard *Rubber Soul* and *Help!* and maybe *Revolver*, my dad would get up and make us frozen pizza. Not only was he safe, but he also didn't know how to cook for shit because he was the best dad ever. We'd sit there in the family room with our pizza on our little card tables and we'd get to watch *The Carol Burnett Show* and laugh and spit pepperoni and drink orange soda like it was the most natural thing in the world. Like it might be next door. There was no fear, no hand-wringing. Saturday was easy except for trying to figure out what John Lennon was upset about.

My dad tried to protect us from my mom, but he couldn't. Lord knows he couldn't protect himself. He could, however, give us Saturdays, and we wished they would last forever.

I hadn't thought about those Saturdays in a very long time until a couple weeks ago when I went to dinner with my friend Ann and her two kids, aged three and five. On the way home she put on a mix CD that her ex made for the kids. First up was the Scorpions' "Rock You Like a Hurricane," then "Holy Diver" by Ronnie James Dio. I looked at Ann in horror, but the kids knew the lyrics to these songs and sang them in their sweet baby angel voices in the back seat. Then Duran Duran's "Girls on Film" came on and they knew the words to that one as well. Ann and I did too, because that one was finally a decent song. We were all screaming "GIRLS ON FILM," dancing in our seat belts and car seats with our hair and arms flying while folks stopped at stoplights wondered what the hell was happening in our car.

When it was over, Ann took that CD out and the kids whined and bitched, but then she pulled *Rubber Soul* out of the CD holder and put it in. I got excited when I heard "Drive My Car" and immediately fast-forwarded to "Norwegian Wood." The bitching stopped. I could tell that they, too, were as intrigued as I had been. The kids sat there silently listening to that instrument and those fascinating lyrics, trying to wrap their little brains around it, drawing pictures in their heads and coming up with their own ideas about why John Lennon was upset.

When I heard that song that night, I was immediately seven or eight or nine. I went back to that little bubble that was Saturday afternoon in the family room of my house. There, it still smells like freshly cut grass and pizza, and my dad is lying on the couch snoring gently with his arms crossed over his chest as if to say, "*I may not be good, but I'm slow, but who gives a shit anyway, because I'm listening to the Beatles and my kids are safe and memorizing songs about sex and arson.*"

Me, I'm sitting on the floor, stopped, looking up at the flecks of dust floating in the late afternoon light, wondering why that song makes me feel funny, wondering what it would be like to actually sleep in the bathtub. I feel safe and watched over. By my dad, by this music.

Photo by: Patricia Lorka

"But Dad, when will you teach me to smoke?"

uncle holly

*P*eople mistake me for a male all the time. More specifically, they mistake me for a fourteen-year-old boy. All I'm apparently missing is that one thing: a skateboard. Come into a public bathroom with me any day and witness the looks on women's faces. If they come in while I'm washing my hands, I can watch them in the mirror as they look at me with concern, then go back and check the sign on the door to make sure they're in the correct one. I assure you, ladies: I can read the sign too.

I've been hanging around with a lot of kids lately because they are magical beings and generally don't give a shit which bathroom I use. They say awesome things at inappropriate times, they dance just because they can't help themselves, and they squeal. When's the last time you were so happy you squealed?

Anyway, I was spending time with a friend who has three great kids and she told them, out of respect and manners, to call me "Miss Holly." Um, that's the grossest thing I've ever heard. Miss Holly sounds so feminine—you can't do that to a person like me. I thought maybe they should call me "Mr. Holly," but that felt equally creepy and made me sound like a science teacher. So, I came up with "Uncle Holly." It's fun and not creepy, and it doesn't imply that I wear either lipstick or a tie clip. Uncle Holly it was.

We went to the public pool in the kids' neighborhood and they started screaming, "Throw me, Uncle Holly," because kids know what real fun is and also how to give adults an accidental workout. When people around us looked at me, wondering why this young man had on a sports bra and couldn't throw these kids for shit, it didn't matter. The kids got it.

Then there was the time a friend came to visit with the kids he'd adopted from Colombia. Excellent kids, these ones. When I met them, I joked to my friend that they, too, should call me Uncle Holly. The kids looked at me, understood completely what was happening, and said, "No. We'll call you Tío Holly." Do I need to tell you that *Tío* means *Uncle* in Spanish? It was perfect.

The only glitch in the weekend was when the oldest of these kids asked me if I had a boyfriend. I told him that no, I liked girls. Without missing a beat, he asked, "Well, do you have a girlfriend?" When I said no, he asked, "Why not?" Look, kid, Tío Holly is having a period of personal growth, okay? Geez.

This has now taken on a life of its own. Three of my friends are pregnant, and they already refer to me as Uncle Holly. Their babies will too. I'll teach all of those kids to drink shitty beer, play horseshoes, and throw a softball—that's what good uncles do.

Photo by: Nevie Owens

fork off

I like nearly everyone else on the planet, have been through my share of difficult breakups. After one of the more spectacular of these breakups, I lost custody of the kitchen table and the spare bed. It was really not that big of a deal in my mind until my parents decided to come visit me for Thanksgiving. Then it became an enormous deal that I had neither a bed for them nor a place to eat. Parents can be pretty needy when it comes to things like sleep and dinner.

I had to think fast. I didn't have extra money to spend on grown-up things like furniture. I needed it for things like Movies On Demand and wine. (Shhh, I was lonely.) I decided instead to call Rent-A-Center. Yes, they had beds and kitchen tables for rent! See, I'm a genius and a problem solver.

When I called them, they asked for the phone numbers of four references. Really, Rent-A-Center? I own both a house and a car, and nobody made any phone calls to check if I'd be responsible enough to handle those items. With lots of scoffing, I gave them two friends (decent senses of humor), my parents (questionable senses of humor, depending on whether the Bills won that day), and my boss (Canadian sense of humor). I politely asked them not to call either my parents or my boss, because what kind of asshat rents a bed and a table? Of course, they called both my parents and my boss to ask if I could be trusted with a stupid bed and table rental.

I very quickly received phone calls from both my parents and my boss, asking if I was doing okay and did I have any problems I wanted to talk to them about? Like maybe I'd developed a gambling habit or was spending all my money on meth instead of household necessities.

Awesome.

Since I wasn't addicted to gambling or drugs, I guess my parents figured I was just a loser who not only couldn't keep a girlfriend but also was struggling in the furniture department, because when they came for Thanksgiving, they brought me a bunch of things they thought I'd need, like dish towels and Christmas plates. Also, forks. They brought me many, many forks. Dad said Mom had hit all the garage sales in town and cleaned them out of all their forks.

I wanted to say, "Mom, the population of my house has just decreased by half. I get by on two forks a week now. I'm all good in the cutlery department." I wondered if she thought that having extra forks would make me more attractive to potential girlfriends. As in, *I live in a world of abundance, ladies. Just open the utensil drawer and see.*

It's a long time later and now I own (own, own, OWN!) both a spare bed and a kitchen table. Also a new dishwasher to wash all my forks. Abundance, I tell you!

a legend on my own bus

You can't make up your own nickname. Everyone knows that. You can't just walk into school one day and announce, "From now on, please refer to me only as Disco." It doesn't work that way. A nickname, like herpes, must be given to you by someone else.

I never wanted herpes, but I always wanted a nickname. Or rather, I always wanted a good nickname. Some of my friends in grade school had them. Dawn Lieber was called Flash. She ran the fifty-meter dash faster than any of the boys. One day our gym teacher yelled out to her, "Go, Flash, go!" and the name stuck. We called her that all the way up through high school, and it always conjured images of supreme athleticism and speed, even though by senior year she weighed over two hundred pounds and smoked weed. And Matt Downy was Hubba. He chewed bubble gum constantly, so we named him after it. He could blow bubbles the size of Jupiter and regularly got the gum stuck in his hair. He laughed every time he was sent to the school nurse to get it out. His mom finally shaved his head.

I was jealous of them. Their unique characteristics made them stand out from everyone else. They morphed into more than just

24

silly little kids with bad perms and bologna sandwiches. They became legendary. Well, I too had a unique characteristic that I thought could make me legendary.

Let's talk about my penmanship: it was amazing.

I was obsessed with handwriting. As a fourth or fifth grader, I felt it was the one individual mark I was capable of making on the world. Perfect penmanship was everything to me. I practiced and practiced with a finely stilettoed #2 Ticonderoga until every letter was the right height, the correct slant. I had a copy of the Bill of Rights in my bedroom, because that was the type of poster I was hanging on my wall at the time. I had it pinned up over my desk, and in the evenings I'd sit and painstakingly copy all the signatures at the bottom, over and over until I knew them by heart. John Hancock was my favorite because he had that "H" in there and it was fucking beautiful.

Every assignment I turned in was given back to me with a comment about how nice and perhaps colonial it looked. Every time I signed my name on my grade school homework the angels sang. If you look at my Social Security card, which my parents let me sign around this time, you might think I was a member of the Constitutional Convention of 1789. Penmanship. That's what I had. This would have been the perfect opportunity for a good nickname. I could have been called Copyright or Inkwell, maybe even Scratch. But that's not what happened.

I was born to two people whose dental histories were savage. My mom lost all of her teeth at a young age to disease and wore complete dentures. I knew this because she would take them out and chase me screeching around the house whenever she wanted a good laugh. Though my dad had most of his own teeth, they were crooked and leaned around in his mouth like drunken sailors. I was fortunate enough to inherit this quality. When my permanent teeth came in, they erupted from my gums in an enamel bouquet, spraying out from my mouth with no regard for order. My upper teeth stuck out so far that I couldn't close my lips over them. The kids on the school bus, recognizing my resemblance to a wood-gnawing rodent, gave me the nickname Bucky Beaver.

The kids on the school bus. The Evil Bus Kids. There were five or six of them, all older than me. Bigger. Meaner. The huddled together in the back, a heaving mass of cackles and pointed fingers, making fun of anyone they could and laughing nonstop at each other's jokes. They were always there, preying on any weakness, any imperfection. I never saw any of them at school, never saw them get on or off the bus. Maybe they lived on the bus. Maybe they toured around from district to district laying siege to kids like me, trying to get us all to cry. They were astute warriors; their most effective weapon was the sharply honed nickname.

Every morning it was the same: when the bus stopped for me in front of my house and opened its doors, I would consider running away to Pennsylvania to live with the Amish people, where all the kids there were homeschooled and never had to ride the bus. While I was planning my escape, the driver would wave me on and tell me that she didn't have all day, honey, and I would realize that I didn't even know where Pennsylvania was. So, steeling myself, I'd climb in. Even though I would rush to get into a seat, looking downward to avoid making eye contact with them, the Evil Bus Kids would start on me immediately.

I was an easy target. Because I couldn't close my mouth over my teeth, my lips were always dry and I developed a habit of licking them constantly. The Evil Bus Kids picked up on this and bestowed upon me another nickname. They squinched up their yellow eyes, pursed their lips, darted their tongues in and out of their mouths, and called me Fofo Face. What even was a Fofo? I didn't know, but it couldn't be good. So, I was Fofo Face Bucky Beaver.

Then I got braces. The Evil Bus Kids just kept tagging on the nicknames. I grew into Fofo Brace Face Bucky Beaver.

My teeth were so bad that I had to wear headgear with my braces. Most kids only had to wear it at night, where its only consequence was an occasional bloody gouging if one turned over too hastily. My orthodontist, however, convinced my parents that my overbite was the worst he'd ever seen. The only way to defeat it was to wear headgear during the day as well.

Kids will notice if you wear a cage on your face in the fourth grade. Especially the Evil Bus Kids. I became Fofo Brace Face Bucky Beaver in a Cage.

Soon after sporting daily headgear, I began having trouble seeing the blackboard. While I was certain that the incarceration of my mouth was interfering with the blood flow to my eyes, the orthodontist assured my mother that the two were not related. Mom took me to the eye doctor, who prescribed glasses for me. When it came time to choose frames, I couldn't get the ones I wanted: an average pair of brown frames with a Battlestar Galactica emblem on the side. That pair wasn't on sale. What was on sale was a pair of pink plastic frames with eyeholes the size of tractor tires. As a bonus, blue tint was included with the lenses. Fantastic! Add that to my orthodontic ensemble and wonder why I didn't just throw myself in front of the bus instead of getting on it every day.

Then, my mom decided I should have a shag haircut. It was stylish in 1977—for adults, maybe even for fashionable teenagers. Not for a fourth or fifth grader like me. My hair was razor-cut to stick up in the top and front; the sides and back hung wispily and seductively over my pink goggles and headgear elastic. I went to school every day while my hair longed to do photo shoots for the cover of *Cosmo*. Everyone else had a regular stupid fourth-grade haircut. I was a freak. "Hey, Fofo Brace Face Bucky Beaver in a Cage with Four Eyes, does Rod Stewart know you have his hair?"

It went on and on, all the way through middle school. I would go home crying to my mom, who would tell me not to worry because those kids would never amount to anything and would someday be pumping my gas. My dad's answer was to take me into the garage and show me how to punch them in the breadbasket if they ever laid a hand on me. But they never touched me. They just ruined my life.

Thanks to the Evil Bus Kids, I became legendary only for my bad teeth and awkward, though somewhat stylish, appearance. I wanted to be memorialized for my handwriting, but how could I convince the Evil Bus Kids? How could I get them to call me something that wasn't completely humiliating? It seemed impossible.

A few years ago, a colleague asked me if I had a nickname. There it was: an opportunity for redemption. A chance to right all the wrongs that were done to me on that stupid bus so long ago. My teeth were straight, my hair looked pretty good, my glasses were acceptable. My handwriting was still perfect. What did I pick? What have I been called now for the last five years at work? My coworkers go into my patients' rooms and tell them what to call me before I introduce myself. When I go in, my patients speak first, to be funny.

They say, "Good morning, Steve."

thug
life

This is the story of fourth grade. Fourth grade is easy for no one, but just look at the picture on the cover of this book and imagine how things were going for me. I was having a huge case of the struggles. I was being bullied for my teeth, my braces, my shyness, my shoes, and my overall existence. I also started writing shit down in notebooks, perhaps to use against people in stories when I got older. Do not fuck with the shy kid who likes English class, you evil bus fuckers.

On the upside, my hair was amazing.

In the fourth grade, I was pretty into my English teacher, Ms. Harmon. She was the first "Ms." I'd ever met. Not a Miss or a Mrs.: far more mysterious, more exotic. Then there was the way she looked. She had long, wavy strawberry blonde hair. She wore colorful muumuus, big gold hoop earrings, and layers of wooden bracelets that clacked together when she wrote vocabulary words on the chalkboard. She had enormous breasts that filled her muumuu and entered the classroom minutes before she did. God, I was so gay for Ms. Harmon. This is probably why I ended up becoming a writer. I longed to lay my head gently upon her ample bosom, correctly spelling words like "eager" and "valiant" while she patted my head with approval. What hot teacher wouldn't want to come home and get motorboated by her ten-year-old star student with amazing bangs?

When I was in the fourth grade, I lived in Nebraska. Lovely Ms. Harmon taught English, and the dreaded Mrs. Payne taught science class. We learned quickly that you'd better not make a joke about Mrs. Payne's name or you were going to the principal's office. She was famous not only for her cranky disposition and her name, but also for the little spitballs she'd get on her lip when she read passages from our science books to us. They'd go up and down with her mouth and we'd all sit there staring at them and wondering why she didn't wipe them off, and if that was going to happen to us when we were elderly forty-year-olds.

She read us the chapter about the planets, about how Saturn is the sixth planet from the sun and the second largest behind Jupiter, and how it has several rings that became visible when Galileo invented the first telescope in 1610. From far away the rings look like beautiful, solid hoops. But in fact, the rings are made out of dust, rocks, and ice that clump together and break apart as they revolve around the yellow planet.

By the fourth grade, most of us had been in the same class for a few years. We sat through insects, food groups, and the solar system together. We could all predict what everyone would bring for lunch each day. We knew that while Mrs. Payne flung her spitballs up and down, Renee was going to ask too many questions, Jimmie was going to smell like pee (thankfully I'd grown out of pants peeing by this time), and Cassie was going to pick her scabs and eat them. Yawn. There was nothing new under our sun.

Then one day after the Christmas break, Becky showed up in our class. Her family had moved to our district from some faraway place called Georgia. We only knew how far away it was because Mrs. Payne pulled down the giant map and pointed it out with her big wooden poker. Georgia was way over there and purple, and Nebraska was here and blue. Becky was dropped down into our midst wearing a pair of overalls and speaking with a southern drawl that was as exotic to us as caviar. We didn't understand, and we were all instantly intrigued.

While most new kids would be shy and quiet, Becky was a firecracker from the get-go. She entertained us with her stories of Georgia roaches "so big you could put a saddle on 'em." She wondered why we didn't have grits in the cafeteria. Um, because we don't even know what grits are. When she said "Go Big Red," "red" grew into a three-syllable word and there was a little kick at the end. She called her dad "Daddy" and her mom "Momma." She always smelled like baked goods, and she could penny-drop like a god. We couldn't stop looking at her or listening to her. We couldn't stay away from her. Gravity drew us to this giant, charismatic shiny object who had magically appeared in our tiny Midwest lives of Pop Rocks and orange drink. Like the rings of Saturn, we little chunks of ice and dust and rock began to orbit around her.

Our school days grew brighter. It was like someone finally changed a giant light bulb that'd been burned out for a long time. Fourth grade was suddenly more than braces and unfortunate haircuts. We all fell into mad crush with Becky, and it made us all insanely happy, as only irrational love can do. Everyone always knew where she was and what she was doing, and we all clambered like hungry little monkeys to be involved as much as possible. We hung around and hung on and became a collective love-struck herd that followed her wherever she went. Poor Becky. We must've been overwhelming, with our desperate desire to suck from her everything that was different from ourselves. But she endured us all with patience, generosity, and joy, which made us love her even more.

Becky's momma was a gospel singer who used to sing back up for Elvis. She even had her own record, and Becky gave us all a copy of it. It was called "I'm Gonna Walk Dem Golden Stairs." We all took our copies home, and to the horror of our parents, played the shit out of that twangy little 45. It must be good music, right? It came from Becky. By March, we knew all the words and would sit on the playground singing, "When Jesus says to me well done, I'll lay down my soul, my battles are won. I'll walk dem golden stairs when I die," in our finest God-fearing Georgia accents. The Nebraskan suburbs had never heard such a thing. Becky sat in the middle of it all, singing along, watching us bump into and climb over each other as we struggled to stay close to her, our yellow Saturn, our new reason for coming to school every day. Becky even began to overshadow my obsession with Ms. Harmon.

And then, just as quickly as she appeared, she vanished. Her daddy was transferred back to Georgia and in an instant she was gone, leaving us alone in the Midwest with just some records and vague ideas about salvation to prove she was ever there. There was mass heartbreak and blank staring. Lots of whining. The giant light bulb was burned out once again. We were blasted out of our reverie, our orbit, our seemingly solid new collective purpose as Becky disciples and wannabe Georgians, only to revert back to what we used to be: just some old pieces of ice and rock, floating around without much purpose, sitting at our gray desks with our unfortunate haircuts, spelling vocabulary words, watching spitballs and eating scabs, listening for the comforting clack-clack of Ms. Harmon's bracelets.

kitchen window

There are a lot of stories about shame in this book. But this story hurts worse than the others, and it all went down while I was standing with my mom in our mustard-yellow kitchen. She was cooking something, which, if she wasn't working or doing laundry, was what she was always doing.

School had just gotten out for the summer, and I walked into the kitchen with my seventh-grade yearbook in my hand. My mom asked how my day was. I said, "Great. Last day of school. We signed yearbooks today. I didn't let Rena sign mine."

Rena and her family lived across the street from us. She was part Asian, which was a big deal in 1983 in suburban Phoenix. It was exotic, and not in a good way. Plus, her last name was K-o-c-h, which was pronounced "cock," so basically, Rena was fucked. But I liked her. She was shy and nice, and sometimes at school we ran in the same circles. The quiet, try-not-to-draw-attention-to-yourself-and-be-killed circles. It's hard to believe, I know, but I was not some incredibly popular seventh grader. I didn't know how to dress, unlike the other girls in their Jordache jeans with their combs sticking out of their back pockets. Every time I tried to carry a comb in my back pocket it would catch the back of my chair when I got up and cause a fiasco. Fiascos don't make you popular until college. Plus, I could never figure out how to use my curling iron correctly, so my hair always looked a little stupid, and my tennis shoes were brown, because they were the only ones that fit my giant feet. An Asian girl named Cock? That was my people.

My parents hated living across the street from a bunch of cocks, and were actually relieved when, years later, a Mexican family moved in.

At Christmastime every year, Mr. Cock grabbed a bunch of colored lights out of the garage and threw them up in his olive tree in the front yard. Like he was setting doves free at a wedding. Except not that majestic. Mostly, it was a shit show, but he didn't care. The lights clumped and dangled, and my father would stare at them through the kitchen window. You could almost smell the disdain bubbling from his eyes. My father was so obsessed with Christmas light perfection that he had drawn blueprints of how they should be put up every year. And when he did, they were so straight and white and perfect they looked like stars had been razor-cut out of the night sky to land on our eaves. And here he was, forced to gaze upon the half-assed nightmare happening across the street. Like Charlie Brown lived there instead of the Cocks.

Rena's father was fat and bald and walked around his front yard in a dirty white tank top, dangling a nasty chewed-up cigar from his mouth and screaming for his kids to pick their shit up, like he was worried about what his yard looked like. His wife was a pretty Asian lady, so my mother concluded that she was a mail-order bride. I imagined my mother would watch them get in the car to go somewhere together and probably think, *They aren't even real,* while drinking another whiskey and yelling at my dad to take out the fucking garbage already. I could tell she was thinking that by the sour look she'd get on her face when she saw them.

Naturally, I thought she'd be pleased when I lied and told her I wouldn't let Rena sign my yearbook. Family solidarity, right? Fuck those Christmas lights. Fuck that front yard yelling. Fuck all those weeds. Fuck the Cocks! But instead, she turned away from her meatballs to look at me and said, "That's mean. You should have let Rena sign it. She's your neighbor."

WHAT?!?

She pointed her finger at me the way she did when she was really pissed. I stood there in the kitchen, looking at the floor, and was covered in shame, like it had steamed out of the vent hood and wafted all over me. Even though I had actually done the right thing without thinking about it because I really liked Rena, I was ashamed that my mom now thought that her own child would actually keep her across-the-street neighbor from signing her yearbook. I was also ashamed that I wanted my mother's approval so much that I would lie and brag about something like that. I had betrayed myself in two different ways, and I was disgusted with myself.

I avoided Rena after that. I couldn't look at her without thinking about what I'd done. When Gilbert eventually moved in with his family, he put candles in paper bags along the driveway instead of hanging Christmas lights. We were all thrilled.

the benefits of being tall and creepy

Near the end of my senior year of high school, I was named Athlete of the Month. I don't think my high school had ever given that award to a girl before. My school was all about football, baseball, and wrestling. Nobody had given a shit about girls' basketball until I made them pay attention.

I had a great year. I high-scored nearly every game, had a free-throw percentage in the 90s, and captured rebounds like I was the only one on the court. I made the newspaper. Colleges took notice (okay, just Yavapai Community College, to be honest). And I did it all for a girl.

The girl was the varsity girls' basketball coach. She was new to our school. She was twenty-two and I was seventeen. She was cute and funny, and during tryouts for the team I saw her and burst into flames, and I made up my mind that not only was I going to make the team, but I was also going to make her love me.

I hadn't even acknowledged yet that I was gay, that every single one of my crushes was on a girl, that I had dreams about kissing girls, that boys grossed me out. It was 1987, and being gay wasn't cool yet. No one was admitting anything.

I made the team, perhaps because I was tall. I certainly wasn't a great basketball player at the start of that season, but I was driven. I had a mission. I was going to be so good that the coach would lose her shit over me.

I ran my suicide drills until my lungs screeched and my legs were about to blow up. I did layups from the right and then from the left like someone possessed. I practiced post shots and free throws until I could make them with my hands tied behind my back. I even learned how to dribble with my left hand. After practice I went home to run and shoot some more, until the driveway went dark. Then I went to bed to construct elaborate fantasies about meeting my coach in the locker room after practice. You'd be surprised how great making out with a basketball coach in a nasty locker room could be in my head.

Surprisingly, I wasn't the only gaybo on the basketball team. It seems you could swing a cat in that locker room and hit seven of us, with our short fingernails and fake purses full of denial. I would only realize how many of us there were when, at the age of twenty-three, I came out and went to the lezzie country bar and systematically ran into nearly every one of my old teammates. *Oh. Hey there . . .*

One of the girls on the team had a mom who was openly gay. Kelly had team parties at her house when her mom was at work. We'd always want to drink and hang out in her mom's bedroom, maybe because there was a poster of a giant sweaty half naked female construction worker hanging above the bed. Maybe. We'd all lie around in there, talking about our fake boyfriends, staring intently at the bead of sweat that would never make it all the way down that poster's cleavage.

Kelly and I became good friends. Not just because I wanted to look at that poster a lot more, but also because we had a few more things in common. She was one of the lezzies, and she, too, was in love with our coach. Neither of us ever admitted it, but we didn't have to. We'd fawn over her together, find reasons to need her help, and get all dopey-faced when talking about her.

Kelly drove a 1976 Trans Am. She'd pick me up and we'd drive that thing all over the city. One night she pulled into a condo complex, parked, and pointed to a second-story window and announced, "That's where the coach lives." Oh, my God. We were at her house! How did she get this information? Who cared—we were here! We sat out there in the dark listening to Billy Idol while looking at her window and talking about everything except why we were there. What a couple of idiots.

I continued to bust my ass at basketball during the day and at night found reasons to drive my shitty Maverick by her complex and pull in and park to watch her window. My locker room fantasies became more elaborate, growing to include a soapy shower and an MVP award that had nothing to do with basketball. I imagined that one night she'd walk out of her condo, see me parked there, and invite me in to use that shower with her. Why the hell wouldn't she? I was out of control and still not admitting to myself that perhaps I was a big homo who was also now a creepy stalker.

My feelings for her were taking over my life. The only outlet for my angst was on the court, where I began to dominate. I poured myself into basketball, and even my dad was surprised at how well I did. It's amazing what you can accomplish when you decide to win someone over with layups. I quickly became the star player, and I knew this would make her love me. Kelly couldn't rebound for shit. Didn't she see? We could have the perfect life together of basketball and soapy showers and home renovation. We could get a dog.

The season passed and we lost some crucial games. We entered the playoffs in poor position and were quickly eliminated. I fouled out of my last game and just like that, it was over. Time was up. The coach and I weren't a couple, she never accidentally took a shower with me in the locker room, hadn't winked at me knowingly, hadn't even patted my bottom the way a coach is supposed to. The season was over, then school was over, and I was out of reasons to be around her. Except at night in my car, which went on for most of that summer until I left for college. (And then a few more times during spring break.)

I ran into her a few years ago. We walked past each other during halftime at a WNBA game. She looked at me and said, "Oh. Hey there." I was immediately back in high school again. I felt my face flush red, my mouth dried up, I lost the ability to speak. I waved and went straight to the bathroom to throw up.

harvest

I arrive at the hospital morgue at 2 a.m. to find the security guard waiting for me as I had requested. In his hands is a large ring of keys. He is already prepared with the key to the morgue grasped between his thumb and forefinger. He quickly unlocks the unmarked metal door, reaches inside to flip on the light, and lets me walk past him to enter the room.

"Do you need anything else?" he asks me, hoping I don't, because he's nervous. He's doing his best to not actually look into the room. In fact, I can tell that he's holding his breath, trying hard not to inhale any of the air that may have escaped when the door opened.

I tell him no, that I'm okay. He nods and closes the door, shuts me in there. I hear his footsteps fading into the hall, and I count them as I look around the room. One, two: the room is small and cold. Three, four: it's very bright, and the fluorescent light bounces off several steel tables. Five, six, seven: there's a sink in one corner, a few cabinets against the walls, a trash can on wheels. Eight: the footsteps fade to nothing as my vision settles on a white plastic shroud lying on top of a gurney in the center of the room. This is why I am here.

The air is still and the room is soundless. As I settle in for my task, I find that every noise I make shatters the silence, reflected and magnified by the steel and the tile. My briefcase peals against the table as I set it down, the clasps bang when I open them, the latex snaps against my skin when I put on gloves. I unzip the plastic shroud and am grateful that the metal whizzes smoothly, without sharpness or echo.

The smell of the body hits me and begins to fill the room as I open the bag. At three hours after death, the odor is not yet sharp or strong. It's dull and sour and creeps in and out of my nose as I work to pull the plastic away from the chest and arms, exposing the ID band that encircles one of the wrists. I verify the name on the bracelet and, satisfied that I have the correct body, proceed.

My parents don't really understand what I do. To be honest, I don't think they want to understand. When I explain that it's better if I can get permission to take out the whole eyeball instead of just the cornea, because then I can excise the cornea in the lab under more controlled conditions, they suddenly become very interested in the evening news. It's okay. I don't really understand why I do it either, except I somehow feel like I'm contributing to society.

I take the instruments from my briefcase and lay them out on one of the steel tables that I've moved next to the gurney. I have a well-rehearsed ritual for arranging the scissors, hemostats, and retractors. Meticulously, almost obsessively, I line them up on the table in the order that they will be used. I don't want to prolong my task with poor preparation, and I feel I owe this person my precision.

I clean the body's face with brown iodine. I start on the lid of each eye and wipe outward in circles of increasing size. The iodine's antiseptic smell is strong, and I use more than is necessary to help disguise the other odors in the room. When I'm through cleaning the skin, I drape the entire face with several blue surgical towels, leaving only the eyes exposed. I pull apart the wet lashes as I raise the lid of each eye, wash the surface with saline, and insert the small retractors to keep them open. I'm trying hard not to think about that scene in *A Clockwork Orange*, which is always what I try not to think of during this part of the procedure. The idea of forcing each brown iris and black pupil to watch what I'm about to do is worse than any scene from a horror film I've ever seen, and I don't even like horror films. I blink my own eyes hard against the thought and do my best to remember that I'm contributing to society.

I maneuver my instruments deftly and remove the clear membrane that covers each eye. I insert my hemostats over the top of one eye, take hold of the muscle that is attached there, and expose it enough to cut it with my scissors. I reach under the eye and grasp it and clip it as I did the other muscle. The eye now floats more freely in the socket, and I can cut the remaining muscles away from the top, the bottom, and the sides. With the eye now released from the muscles that held it in its socket, I have room to reach around behind it with the special long, curved scissors to sever the tough optic nerve. The eye is now completely free, and I carefully lift it out and place it in a clear glass jar for transport back to the lab. I repeat the same procedure with the other eye and hope I don't get pulled over and searched on my way back to the lab, because there would be a lot of uncomfortable explaining.

At this point I could remove the blue drapes, but I don't, because I would most likely run screaming from the room. The gaping sockets are easier to handle with the drapes on, when it isn't quite a face. The smells drift in and out of my nose, I can hear myself breathing, and I'm looking into the empty eye sockets of a dead person. In the morgue. Alone. In the middle of the night. This is the birthplace of ghosts and hauntings. This is when I'm really scared.

There was a time when I was able to harvest a person's eyes while he was still up in the ICU, which I was incredibly relieved about because there'd be other alive people and activity around me.

Then the nurse put the head of the patient's bed down after I'd taken out his eyes, and the deceased let out a giant exhale. You know that feeling you get when you accidentally run over a baby in your car? Well, I felt about a million times worse than that until the nurse laughed at me and told me it was just from the change in lung pressure when she put the bed down. "Don't worry, honey. He's dead."

He's dead. So, empty eye sockets alone in the middle of the night in the morgue or not, I resolve to continue. I reach for the small green rubber balls that I have with me and place one in each empty socket before removing the retractors and closing the lids. I've traded my counterfeits for what were once bright brown eyes, and when I'm through, when the lids are once again closed, I finally remove the drapes to view the face. I make sure the prosthetics are positioned properly to give the lids a natural appearance. When I'm satisfied they are, I wash off the iodine and leave the face as it was before I arrived. He looks serene and forgiving, so I reciprocate by sticking a giant needle into this man's chest where I know his heart is. I need a blood sample to test for infectious diseases back at the lab, and the heart is the only place you can draw blood from someone who is dead. What the hell kind of job is this anyway? For someone who is twenty-one and hopeful and sensitive and doesn't like horror films because they're too scary? I wish they'd told me this part of it before I accepted the job. It might've been what made me say, "Nah, thanks anyway."

I do the "in the heart" blood draw as reluctantly as I would run over another baby in my car, and I am officially done.

Relieved, I silently thank this man for donating his corneas and zip the shroud closed. I pack up my things, wash my hands, open the door to the rest of the hospital, and turn off the light and leave.

I took this job at the eye bank harvesting corneas while I was in nursing school. Being on call at night worked well with my classes.

I didn't realize how many people died in the middle of the night or how horrifying they'd look without their eyes. I managed to do it for six months before the smell of my lab coat and the act of driving the city streets of Phoenix at night with eyeballs in my Toyota pickup became too much. I quit to go wait tables at a Mexican restaurant. Serving chips and queso to hungry people is contributing plenty to society, okay?

what i didn't consider when i went to nursing school

*J*anet Sinclair had the loudest laugh that anyone around her had ever heard. Her husband said she could go from zero to full-out screaming laugher in nothing flat and it would scare the crap out of you if you weren't expecting it. He said that was his favorite thing about her.

She liked to watch softball games and would go to see her niece play and holler from the stands. She listened to country music, had every George Strait album, and liked to two-step. That's how she met Jeff: he asked her to dance at Toolie's. They got married a year later, and now she was pregnant with their first baby.

At twenty-five, Janet was just one year older than I was. Under normal circumstances, we might have hung out, drank beer, and screamed at softball games together. We might have been friends. Under normal circumstances, I wouldn't have had to put her into a body bag and then go home to get drunk at 7 a.m.

The night I met Janet, I was just six months into my nursing career. I worked in a busy cardiovascular ICU, where many of the patients were elderly folks who had open-heart surgery. Most did very well. They'd pat my hand and eat Jell-O when they healed, and I'd get to smile and hang up my stethoscope proudly before I punched out each morning. Sure, I had taken care of a few people with serious problems, but I was generally assigned the more stable cases. By nursing standards, I was still just a rookie.

That all changed when I met Janet. It was one of those nights when no one sat down, when every patient on the unit had significant problems, when there was a full moon shouting "DANGER" through every window. There was a loud beep-beep from the computer, two exclamation points of sound while it spit out an admit slip: a young pregnant woman was in surgery having an emergency C-section. She'd be coming to us with a severe case of sepsis. She was crashing, and I was the only one free enough to take her. The charge nurse told me this as she handed me the slip with more than a little concern on her face. I smelled the sweat of pure fear erupt under my new blue scrubs. No one would be eating Jell-O tonight.

Janet hadn't been feeling well for a few days. She thought it was just fatigue from being pregnant for so long and believed that her cough was from allergies. She was at a softball game that night, sitting in the bleachers hollering her fool head off when her back started to hurt. It got so bad Jeff forced her to come to the hospital.

She had pneumonia, and by the time she came to the hospital the infection had spread to her blood. Her baby was delivered and doing fine, but Janet was in trouble. She rolled into our unit with a breathing tube and very little blood pressure, so we had to start her on high doses of IV medications to raise it to a viable level. I was busier and more challenged than I ever had been, helping to place a central line, drawing labs, trying to keep Janet stable, trying to keep myself from crashing under all of the pressure. Somehow, we both made it through the night.

I worked four nights in a row after admitting Janet and was assigned to her each night. Though she remained on the ventilator, she improved dramatically. We stopped her sedation after the second night and allowed her to wake up. The first question she mouthed to me around her breathing tube was, "How is my baby?"

Her baby was fine. Jeff brought their daughter into the unit. Since we couldn't allow him to bring her into Janet's room because of the risk of infection, he would stand holding her outside the window. Janet could see her from there and would wave, reaching her hand out, trying to touch her baby through the glass. For those of us used to caring for elderly patients, having a baby on the unit was alien. That little girl's presence was magic; it pulled all of us out of our sometimes mechanical roles as nurses and turned us into people. Janet and Jeff and their daughter became our temporary family.

By my third night with her Janet seemed like she was out of the woods. Her pneumonia was still bad enough to necessitate the breathing tube, but her body was responding well to the antibiotics. We weaned her off all the blood pressure medication, and she was mouthing words around her tube and writing notes to us when she needed to.

Her personality came out. She smiled all the time, wrote us stupid knock-knock jokes, and teased her husband about how awful he looked. She was ruthless and I loved her for it. Because I worked at night, we had lots of time to talk about her life and mine. She'd graduated from the same high school that my girlfriend had, and we both played basketball. I told her I liked country music, so she promised that we would meet up at Toolie's and her husband would teach me how to two-step. Everyone on the unit got a huge kick out of her. All the nurses, from both the day and night shifts, would find excuses to stop by her room and visit.

Jeff was around as much as he could be. He spent a lot of his time upstairs with his daughter but brought her down to peek at Mom through the window when he could. Jeff turned Janet's hospital room into a carnival. He taped a million pictures of their new daughter around the room, hung up cards and letters from friends and family, and brought balloons in every day. He plugged in a boom box and played George Strait over and over. The only thing that reminded anyone it was an ICU room was the ventilator.

After four nights with Janet, I had three nights off. I used that time to try to stop singing "Amarillo by Morning" in my head. When I walked back onto the unit, I immediately headed for Janet's room to see how she was. The breathing tube was gone and she was sitting up in a chair. She smiled at me and said, "Well, hello." It was the first time I heard her speak. The number of pictures and cards on the walls had doubled, and the George Strait was still playing. I told her that she really needed to get some new music.

She pointed to a Polaroid on her bedside table. It was of Janet holding her baby girl for the first time. "Jeff snuck her in to see me yesterday. Isn't she just beautiful?" They were both beautiful.

About eleven o'clock, she called me into her room and said that she felt short of breath. Her oxygen level was good, but I increased the flow a bit to keep her comfortable. I listened to her lungs, which sounded coarser than before, so I sat her up in bed and ordered a breathing treatment. Neither the extra oxygen nor the treatment helped; her respiratory rate increased and oxygen level dropped. I ordered some blood tests and called her doctor with the results. According to the tests, her infection was worsening.

I had heard about nurse's intuition, about how sometimes you can just know in your gut what will happen to a patient. It hadn't ever happened to me before that night, but there it was: a solid slab of granite pushing my insides down toward the center of the earth, burying my newness beneath it. Janet was twenty-five years old, had just had a baby, was a smart-ass, listened to country music, and had everything good in her life to look forward to, but she wasn't going to get any better. She would never meet me out to go two-stepping. I stood there that night with her test results in my hand, looking in at her and at all the pictures of her baby girl through that window, and I knew she was going to die. That was the first time I cried at work.

I called Jeff at home and told him to come in. I didn't get into details with him, but he knew by the tone in my voice that it was serious. I walked in to tell Janet the results of her tests, wearing the severity of her situation on my face. She saw it, registered it, and then apologized for keeping everyone awake.

Janet's condition worsened rapidly. Within an hour she was sitting straight up in bed clutching the side rails. Her respiratory effort intensified and erupted in beads of perspiration over her lip and across her forehead. We needed to help her by reinserting the breathing tube.

The intubation was difficult. I gave Janet narcotics to help relax her, then held her hand while first the intern and then the resident worked to place the breathing tube. It did not go smoothly and it took a long time. During the procedure I watched the monitor and reported Janet's oxygen saturation as I was trained to do. I saw it plummet from 80 percent down to 40 percent. The doctors were struggling while I called out the numbers. When it hit 27 percent, I looked down at Janet. Her face was blue.

I hadn't ever seen anyone die before. I had heard stories about what it was like from some of the other nurses, but I hadn't had it happen on my shift yet. I expected that when it did happen it would be someone old and frail, someone who had lived a long life, someone I didn't know or care about. That's how I wanted it to be.

But this was Janet. She was young and full and real to me. I cared deeply about her. Seeing her face right then, blue and fading in the absolute light of the ICU, sent the reality of her death charging into me. I was an unsuspecting pedestrian, hit by a semi-truck in the middle of the night.

In the next instant, the resident placed the breathing tube and

Janet's oxygen level increased rapidly. We all stepped back and nearly collapsed from the weight of what had nearly happened, knowing that we had gotten very lucky. I gathered my innards into a pile, stuffed them back into my uniform, and finished the shift. At 7 a.m., when I was getting ready to leave, Janet was lucid enough to communicate. With a clipboard held under her right hand she wrote, in shaky letters that nearly trailed off the page, "It's OK." I touched her forehead, told her I'd see her that night, and made it out of the room before I cried again.

I came back that night to care for her. I went into her room, and the sight of her stripped me down to the bone. Her face had swollen to three times its normal size, and the skin over her cheeks was taut and shiny like polished stone. Her tongue had grown too large for her mouth and lolled out and around the breathing tube. Her eyelids had swollen open to leave her staring out at us and at the pictures of her daughter around her. I didn't want to see her that way, didn't want to be a witness. I turned away from her, hiding the cruelty of my naked horror and grief from her vacant eyes.

She was unresponsive. Her husband was at her bedside holding her hand.

Janet coded at 11:30 that night. We tried for four hours to save her. At one point, I counted eleven IV pumps running wide open, trying to deliver something to keep her alive. My fingers were red and sore from dialing dosages into them, always up, up, up. We worked frantically, surrounded by the pictures of her baby looking at us, silently begging us to do something more. There was nothing more we could do. The doctor who was running the code whispered into the silence of our bent heads, "That's it. I have to call it."

Jeff sat beside his wife for a long time in the dark. He held her hand and stooped his head to cry heavily into her. His sobs spread out from him in massive waves that crashed out of the room and filled the entire unit. We were all engulfed in it, and as it mixed with our own grief, we were pulled under to a place where we couldn't stand or breathe.

He exhausted himself to stillness, then got up, turned the lights on, and slowly took down all the pictures and cards, placing each item into an empty washbasin. I came in and quietly helped him pack up the rest of her belongings. Before he left the room for the last time, he turned to me as if he had just then remembered something. That's when he told me about how it was when she laughed.

I stayed in her room, disconnecting her IVs, cleaning her, getting her body ready to be transported. I could smell the morning coffee being brewed in the unit and knew with a spike of anger and loss that there would soon be another patient coming to take Janet's room.

When I was done with her, I looked around at the walls one last time and saw that Jeff had left something. There was a small piece of paper still taped to the wall. It said, in Janet's handwriting, "Jennifer Elizabeth Sinclair." The name of her daughter.

I took that piece of paper down, put it in my pocket, and walked out of the room to go home and get drunk.

happy valentine's day

/ lost my virginity on Valentine's Day to someone named Walter. This was long before I became brave enough to venture out into Homoville, so it was Walterville first. In a fair world, that name would have been the worst part about him, but it wasn't. He was pudgy and pale and had curly hair that he gelled back tightly on the sides while leaving the rest crunchy atop his head like tiny danger springs. He had perfectly groomed facial hair that he trimmed too high up his neck, like we couldn't tell where his chin really ended. He had a tic that made him sniff all the time.

This was the guy I chose to give myself completely to, to cross the field of dreams with. I was nineteen and tired of not having done it. This was America, for God's sake, and I was clearly behind my horny peers who had all slid into home plate if not by prom, then at least by high school graduation. I was finally ready for glory, and Walter was the safe, soft vessel I chose to deliver me there.

He took me to see Sting in concert. Back in college, I loved Sting. It was his *Nothing Like the Sun* era when he grew his hair out. It was soft and seductive, and on the album cover he was running his fine artistic hand through it while pouting in a dark turtleneck.

He was beautiful, so of course I had a huge crush on him. Walter knew this and busted out his one cool move in life: he got the two of us tickets to see him perform on Valentine's Day.

I would reward him for that.

I decided before he picked me up at my sister's house that I was going to give it up that night. I shaved my legs and told my sister I was going to have sex with the guy who picked me up. I'm sure when she opened the door and saw who was standing there, sniffing away on her porch, she thought I was a complete idiot. But he had those tickets.

The concert was amazing, and afterwards we went back to the apartment Walter shared with his brother. He took me into the bedroom he shared with his brother, removed the mattress from the top bunk of the bunk beds he shared with his brother, and put it on the floor so we could be more comfortable. I want to assure you that no, Walter was not ten years old. He was twenty-four.

When it happened, as he was fumbling and clambering, sweating all over me and handing me one of the worst sexual experiences of my life, I distinctly remember thinking two things. First: I'd always remember Valentine's Day as the day I lost my virginity. And second: I'd always remember losing my virginity to an unfortunate man named Walter, on the floor, on his bunk bed mattress. That shit just doesn't go away.

Fast-forward a few years to when I was planning my first Valentine's Day with my fiancée, Gary. It was my first one to celebrate with someone since Walter, and I wanted it to be different. I wanted it to be romantic and hot and enjoyable. I wanted to get Gary something nice. He treated me well. He went to Paris on business and brought me back expensive French perfume. He took me out to the desert to four-wheel and shoot beer cans. He was a gentleman, so I got him the best thing I could think of. What I thought anyone would want to get for Valentine's Day. I got him blow job porn.

I couldn't wait for that day to roll around, because we were going to watch blow job porn, and I was going to have the best Valentine's Day ever. Watching blow job porn was my secret favorite thing to do, despite the time I gave an awkward beej in the back of the Pontiac years before. I remember the first time I saw it. I was twelve or thirteen, and my parents had just gotten cable TV. The Playboy Channel was scrambled, but every once in a while, if you were lucky, when you quietly turned to channel 37 while everyone else was busy or gone, it would unscramble long enough to make out a boob. A BOOB! Then the picture would distort again, and you could get back to the rest of your day. This particular time, however, I got luckier than I had ever imagined. The squiggles disappeared, the pixels all lined up, and the whole picture came into focus, as clear as *The Price Is Right* on channel 5. But Bob Barker was nowhere in this scene.

Instead, a man with his pants off was sitting on the keys of an upright piano. There was a naked blonde woman kneeling in front of him, and she had his penis in her mouth. She was blowing his lights out while the piano keys made clumped-together noise underneath him. HOLY SHIT! There it was, right there. This thing that I didn't even know I liked. This way of sex that I'd heard about from kids on the bus but hadn't gotten a great visual on yet. SHE HAD IT IN HER MOUTH! Right there in the living room!

It was unexpectedly SO much better than seeing just a boob. It set my skinny, adolescent body on fire. I immediately shoved my hand down my pants and came about sixteen times before it scrambled again to leave me alone in my living room. Changed. Messy.

What was it, exactly, about watching this scene that set me off the way it did? I had known I wanted to be a boy for a while now, sure. But now I knew that I wanted somebody to do that to me. I knew that, specifically, I wanted to be the man with the penis in that scene. I wanted to be there while a naked woman with big boobs liked me enough to get on her knees in front of me and put that excellent part of me in her mouth. I knew that I also played the piano, and I could go sit on it right now.

From that day on, I was obsessed with blow jobs, with a girl kneeling in front of me like that. It's what I thought about every single time I whacked off. It's what I dreamed about. It's what I thought about when I started having sex with men and let them go down on me. It's what I wanted to watch a whole bunch more but couldn't, until I moved out of my parents' house and into Gary's. He had a VCR. I was a grown-up. I could do whatever I wanted, and the thought of just blatantly buying and then watching my favorite thing ever was exhilarating. If I wanted to go, uncomfortably, into the adult bookstore and ask for recommendations about which blow job porn tape was the best to give to my fiancée for Valentine's Day—well, I could, couldn't I?

I gave that to Gary with a straight face. I guess he went about purchasing his gift for me in the same fucked-up way that I did, because you know what he gave me? He, with a straight face, gave me a purple teddy. Because that's what HE wanted: a girlfriend who wore a purple teddy to bed. That's probably what he thought about when he whacked off. Maybe he saw something like that on the Playboy Channel when he was twelve, and it stayed forever cemented in HIS dirty little mind.

Go to the back of this book and look at my picture. How do you think I looked in that teddy? Well, I assure you it was exactly that bad. It was not a garment meant for a tall girl. The thong part that was supposed to look ever-so-sexy just almost cut me in half. Hunched over to make myself shorter and lessen the trauma, I lumbered out of the bathroom a cross-dressed horny maniac who couldn't wait to roll the porno.

There we were on that romantic fantasy Valentine's Day night with the light from *Babes in Blowland* flickering against the bedroom walls. Me, wearing that purple atrocity and trying to act all kitten sexy just so he'd go down on me—during a good blow job scene, so I could watch it and pretend that he was a pretty girl with a nice rack instead of an insanely hairy straight guy who had my imagined penis in his mouth and was letting me come on his face.

Happy Valentine's Day!

And it was. We had a lot of sex that night. I bet he wondered what the fuck happened to make me so turned on. I bet he planned to purchase a bunch of other teddies for me to wear. Poor Gary. He had no idea he was sucking my enormous secret dick. I sure as fuck wasn't going to tell him.

I wore him out. He spoke with a lisp for days. But when he fell asleep that night I still wasn't satisfied. I wanted to watch more of that porn, because it was there and it was my scary secret fantasy. I felt like an alcoholic who lies sweaty in bed at night and remembers that she has a bottle of vodka stashed in the washing machine. I couldn't stop thinking about it. PORN, PORN, PORN. When I knew he was good and asleep, when his snoring got loud, I snuck the movie downstairs to the other VCR and watched it and whacked off some more. God, was this even legal? It was certainly the best Valentine's Day anyone had ever had!

Thus my love affair with porn, specifically blow job porn, was sealed. I got older and my life changed in a lot of ways, but this one thing never did. It's still my fantasy, though no longer scary and definitely not a secret. But I've only told this whole story one other time.

I was at the adult store. I picked out two movies, probably something like *Headed to Headland* or, let's just admit it: *BlowBang Seven*. When I took them up to the counter to check out, the clerk looked me up and down, then looked at the movies and said, "Hey. You're a lesbian, right?" (I was probably wearing the standard baseball hat and cargo shorts of my people circa 2007.) "What's with the blow jobs?"

First, I'm pretty sure there's never supposed to be any talking in the porn store. It's, like, the quietest place ever. I mean, you shouldn't even look at anyone, let alone talk to them. And second, can you even imagine what this guy has seen cross his counter? Gangbang rope bondage, fishnet foot job porn, hairy granny porn, piss porn, tickle porn, midget porn, Appalachian bukkake, zombie anal fisting, and other stuff that I can't even think up right now. And he's questioning me about standard hctcro blow jobs?

So I told him everything. I told him about wanting to be a boy, about my penis envy, about that scene I saw in my adolescent living room, about wanting a girl to do that, about Valentine's Day with Gary. I told this porn clerk all of my secrets.

For the record, don't ever do that, because I guess that made us friends. He felt like he should tell me all of his secrets. Apparently, he had fucked every porn actress in the movies on this one shelf over here, his "Special Shelf," and told me he'd had so much sex he wouldn't even bother talking to a girl if she didn't do anal. I remember thinking, *Well, that must make it difficult to order at the drive-through.* I carefully picked up my black plastic bag and backed out of the store.

While porn will always be my good friend, it'll never ever be like it was that first time in my parents' living room, the day that naked blonde woman blew the shit out of that guy with the handlebar moustache on the piano. I haven't thought about that day in a long time, about how powerful that was. Writing this story took a long time because I got so horny thinking about it, I had to keep stopping to go watch more porn and whack off. It's incredible how things we see for the first time in our adolescent fervor can affect who we are for the rest of our lives. I'm just glad the Playboy Channel gave me a blow job scene that day and not a zombie anal fisting one.

you've got a friend

I don't have blinds on many of my windows because I have never been overly concerned with privacy. If you want to look into my house at night and see me sitting on the couch watching HGTV in my skull and crossbones Santa sleeping pants, have at it. Just don't make the Chihuahuas bark, because I'm sick of listening to them bark, which I should've considered before I got two little ~~Chihuahuas~~ barking machines.

There is a window over my desk that looks out into the backyard, and through it I can see the utility pole that holds the power lines. I spend a lot of time staring out at this pole and these lines, because there's nothing keeping me from doing it and because that's how exciting writing can be.

One day I looked out and there was a red stuffed bear sitting high up on the power lines near the pole. The fuck? Writing done for the day.

No, really. There was a red teddy bear sitting up there looking at me through my window, like *Hey, Holly, what's up?* I took a picture because I knew no one would believe me, but it was with my flip phone, so I'm pretty sure that picture is gone forever. But I assure you, that bear was definitely there.

How the hell did a teddy bear get up on my power lines? It was easily thirty feet in the air. The pole is in the corner, engulfed in bamboo. There's no alley, so someone would've had to come into my yard to access it. I googled "unusual electrician rituals" to see if maybe those guys like to mess with people by putting things up there when they work on the lines. Good one, guys. But there was nothing on the Internet about this. I can tell you with certainty that no one had been in my yard. The little barking machines let me know if even a beetle shows up unannounced. Person in yard climbing pole to plant stuffed bear equals major barking bonanza.

It couldn't have been tossed up there—it was wedged too tightly. I considered all the possibilities, none of which was even remotely reasonable, and came up empty.

Regardless of how unreasonable it was, that bear stayed up there for over a year. Through wind and rain, with possums and squirrels climbing over him and bamboo tickling his undercarriage, he just sat up there looking at me through my naked window. He saw me through some cold and lonely times of personal growth, huddled around a cup of tea, pining away for all kinds of silly things. He watched me during some frustrating ones, where I'm sure he wondered why I banged my head on my desk so much (because I'm a writer, bear), and saw me through some triumphant ones, like when I finally learned how to play "Never Going Back Again" on my guitar, which is a really fucking difficult thing to do. I jumped up and down in front of him that day and set the Chihuahuas to barking, which immediately ruined the moment.

Those fucking dogs.

He turned less and less red, to more of a pink, with the weather beating on him. He also got smaller as he lost stuffing and other body parts, but I came to take great comfort in his odd presence. It was just another thing in my life that was strange and unanswerable, but also kind of nice if I didn't think about it too much.

One day, just as suddenly as he appeared, he was gone. I guess that's how it is with something like a fall from the power lines. There's no way to make that happen gradually. Goodbye, bear. It was fun while it lasted.

I didn't go looking for him. It's messy back there in the bamboo. I don't like beetles and possums, and also there are a lot of snails that crunch when you accidentally walk on them. No, thank you. I moved on and started staring at the dead branch stuck up in the chinaberry tree.

Then, some tree limbs that were not dead fell back there (the live ones fall all the time, but I can't get the dead ones to fall even if I promise them candy and puppies), and when I cleaned them up, I FOUND THE BEAR! Or what was left of him, which was his head with just a right arm attached. My little bear! I picked him up like a kid who just found his long-lost stuffed bear, except I was middle-aged, so it happened more slowly and my hands weren't as sticky.

I'd never seen his face this closely. I guess I always assumed he was smiling at me from the power line; it was too far for me to tell for sure. But he was smiling now, even though he was missing a bunch of skin off his nose. He was ragged but he was cute, and he was mine.

I hammered a nail in my porch and I securely hung up what was left of him, because I didn't want to lose him ever again. It may seem silly, but he means that much to me, that little bear. And he fits right in with all the other weird shit I have hanging around my house. I like to drink beer back there with the Christmas lights on while we watch each other and listen to the ~~motherfucking barkers~~ Chihuahuas. It makes me so damned happy that this strange thing happened and that now I can keep this little bear, my odd inanimate friend, here with me. If you know how this little bear got up on those power lines, please never tell me. I'd rather just enjoy the mystery and not think too much about it.

in bed
with
buck owens

*T*he banjo: a five-stringed wood and steel monster that melds the sounds of guitar and drum into one thundering peal, the only instrument to originate in North America, the epitome of the South, the driving force of bluegrass music, the main character in at least one terrifying movie about four men and a river.

Stacey was my first serious relationship. We met while working the night shift at a big hospital. I walked by her, and she looked up at me and smiled her enormous smile. I was immediately hooked. I just happened to have a vacancy in the pretty, tall, redhead department. Her resemblance to Stefanie Powers was uncanny. Don't judge us for this, but many a night was spent making out in patient bathrooms, because Stacey had kids and not a lot of free time, and we were being as efficient with our romance as possible. Efficient but apparently not very discreet: one of the other nurses pulled me aside to ask, "So, are you gnawing on Stacey or what?" Night-shift nurses are a special type of classy.

Stacey gave me my first banjo, so I blame this story on her. I started playing it after her father died. He bought it on a whim and picked at it only casually. Mostly it sat in his closet, behind the wool blazer he wore to funerals. After he died of colon cancer, Stacey gave his banjo to me.

When I was a kid I watched *Hee Haw* with my family. What wasn't there to like about that show? It had stupid jokes, dogs, and farm girls in miniskirts. The other thing it had was banjo music. *Hee Haw* was my first exposure to that instrument, and I was obsessed. My parents gave me an orange plastic banjo for Christmas, and I'd sit in front of *Hee Haw* with it, impatient for some banjo music to come on so I could pretend I was playing along with them, maybe with one of those farm girls on my lap. I'm sure my New Yorker parents were horrified. It was good practice for all the other times I'd horrify them throughout their lives. Poor parents.

When I inherited Stacey's father's banjo, I was delighted. It brought me back to those Saturday nights as a kid, sitting there and pretending. Now, maybe, I could learn to play it for real. I immediately signed up for lessons down at Ziggie's guitar shop, bought some finger picks, strummed my first open G-chord, and fell madly in love. My God, it was so loud and beautiful.

After my first lesson, I went home and started to play. The metallic staccato rolled out of the instrument, crawled up under my skin, and infected me. I was hooked. I began to practice all the time. I developed calluses on my fingers and the muscles required to keep the heavy monster hoisted on my shoulder. I picked my forward rolls, reverse rolls, and multiple measure rolls until they were perfect. I learned hammer-ons, pull-offs and slides. Every night after work I shut myself in the bedroom and played until my fingers nearly fell off. Stacey said that she would leave me if she had to listen to "Boil Them Cabbage Down" one more time, but I couldn't stop. Playing was methodical, rhythmic, meditative. I practiced so hard that the rest of the world fell away, and I was left by myself, mouth open, drooling.

The banjo began to interfere with my life. At work I'd lose

track of what I was doing and find myself silently tapping out the patterns to "Old Joe Clark" or "Cripple Creek" or whatever song I was learning. I stopped watching all of my favorite TV shows so I could have more time to listen to music and practice. I bought every bluegrass CD I could find and memorized all the banjo parts in my head. I studied the lives of Earl Scruggs and Paul Stanley. I wanted to be like them. I stopped going to weekend barbecues so I could go to bluegrass festivals instead. I bought a straw hat.

I sped through my entire lesson book in three months. I had devoured the chords, the scales, and the songs, and, like a junkie, I wanted more. My instructor told me he had nothing left to teach me.

"Where do I go from here?" I asked him.

"I don't know," he said. "None of my other students ever finished." I was on my own.

I started going to bluegrass jams to find others like me. What I found, in suburban Phoenix, were skinny old men with dirty fingernails who chain-smoked while debating the legitimacy of claw hammer and the role of gospel in modern bluegrass music. They played "Foggy Mountain Breakdown" like gods; they wielded banjos instead of thunderbolts. I sat in awe and pitifully tried to keep up. They were sweet and took the time to teach me new chords, new licks. My obsession intensified.

I learned things, secret things that only banjo players know. I learned to turn the phone off while playing. Finger picks don't work for shit on a phone, and taking them off repeatedly is annoying. I learned that dogs flee from the sound and even the sight of my banjo while cats are drawn to it. I learned never to practice in any room near the front of the house because banjo music finds its way under doors and through windows to run amok in the neighborhood and proselytize to innocent joggers and dog walkers.

My friends began taking great pleasure in teasing me about what a hillbilly I'd become since this whole banjo business started.

Maybe it was the straw hat. One of them got me a washboard for my birthday as a joke. I had to explain that the washboard is a totally different category of instrument than a banjo, asshole.

I lost a lot of sleep over the banjo. The nightmares kept waking me up. I dreamed that my backyard turned to swamp and teemed with flies and hungry alligators. Then, I was in bed with Buck Owens. He didn't want to have sex; he just wanted to play "Dueling Banjos." I used to wake Stacey up to tell her.

"Why don't you just stop playing?" she asked. But I couldn't. Not any more than I could wake her dad from the dead and give his instrument back. Not any more than I could stop breathing. The banjo was in me.

poseur with casserole

"*T*hat was my first concert. Wasn't it great?" The girl taking my order for an iced Americano is smiling and waiting for me to answer.

"Huh?" That's all I can say. I have no idea to which concert she's referring. I'm pretty sure our conversation up to this point has only been about coffee. She looks at my chest and points.

"Your shirt."

I finally realize she's referring to the Pearl Jam concert T-shirt I'm wearing. It's from their 1997 show with the Rolling Stones at the Oakland Coliseum. It probably was a great concert, but I wasn't there. "Your shirt," she says again, like I didn't hear her the first time.

"Um. Yeah! It was a great show!" I'm enthusiastic, but I'm also avoiding her eyes and looking at the counter to hide the fact that I'm lying.

Like I said before, I didn't go to that concert. In fact, I haven't been to any Pearl Jam concerts. I bought the shirt at a secondhand clothing store. I saw it hanging there and it called to me. It was black and worn and the red yield sign on the front of it was just starting to fade in that good way that smacks of vintage. "Buy me,"

65

it whispered, "and you can pretend to be someone else." Its words rolled out and over me slowly and gnawed at my longing to fit in with a different group of people.

I do like to listen to music and I do go to some concerts. But I don't buy T-shirts to commemorate my presence at these events because I don't want to advertise my interest in them. It wouldn't be cool to wear a shirt from the Junebug Music Festival and Country Carnival. I'm embarrassed by my musical tastes, but I can't help them. I have a few Indigo Girls shirts lying around, but mostly I wear them to do yard work these days. There's no need to wear them in public.

This was back in the early 2000s, so bear with me. What that shirt offered me back then was that when I wore it, I would look like someone who went to the most awesome Pearl Jam concert ever, in a coliseum, no less. What the shirt didn't tell me, however, was how stressful it would be to keep up the act.

It began the first time I wore it. I was at the bike shop buying new handlebar streamers. I couldn't help that, either. The guy behind the counter looked at my shirt and said, "Dude. That was the best concert ever. I wish they'd put out some better music now. But nothing will ever touch *Ten*, don't ya think?" Would you ask that question to a thirty-five-year-old buying handlebar streamers for her bike?

Now, I knew a little about Pearl Jam. I listened to the radio a bit in the '90s and could tell you that there was a song called "Even Flow" that I kind of liked. I knew they were from Seattle, and I could also tell you that Eddie Vedder was the lead singer. What I didn't know, however, was what *Ten* was or if anything could touch it or not. I had to lie. I said, "Dude. Nothing will ever come close to *Ten*. Can I have my streamers?"

The next time I wore it was in New Orleans. I was walking down Bourbon Street in the midst of a huge crowd, when a girl wearing big black boots and a beret walked up to me and gave me the official rock-and-roll salute, the sign of the horns. I figured she just thought I was cool, but then she said it.

"That concert kicked total ass!"

Did everyone on the planet but me go to that concert?

It happened almost every time I wore it. I'd just be standing there in it, trying to look cool, trying to act like I'm on the cutting edge of at least one thing, when I'd get ambushed by someone who liked to say "dude" or made funny hand gestures that I don't really understand or had lots of things pierced. I finally had to get on the Internet and do some research about Pearl Jam so I could participate in a conversation about them. This is how far I was willing to go just so I could wear that stupid T-shirt. There wasn't much about that particular concert, however. So if someone wanted to chat specifically about that *incredibly important* night in history, I just acted really excited, used the word "dude," and made a hasty getaway.

One evening I was in line at the grocery store. It was the snooty grocery store, the one where olives are really expensive. A guy behind me in the checkout line tapped me on the shoulder and said, "That was, like, the best show ever. What's your favorite CD?"

As usual, I forgot that I was wearing the shirt and wanted to reply, "My favorite CD is Dolly Parton's *The Grass Is Blue*." It took me a minute to realize he was talking about my shirt. They were always talking about that stupid shirt.

I couldn't take it anymore. I was tired of the lying, tired of the facade. I broke down and told him, "Look. I didn't go to the concert. I don't even like Pearl Jam all that much. I bought it at a secondhand store because I thought it was cool."

He looked me dead in the eye. He peeled me down to my very being with his eyes and held me there, naked. "So you're just a poseur, then."

As he turned away from me, I stood there, blinking at him,

with the smell of old bananas in the air and the beep-beep of the laser scanners going off around me. I was sure that everyone in the store could see what he had just done to me, what I had done to myself.

Yes, I am a poseur, in every sense of the word. I've been trying since I can remember to fit into some idealized notion I have for myself of being a cool human on this planet. I'm never cool enough, though. I have tattoos and a pompadour, but I drive a Hyundai, not a motorcycle, as people often assume (motorcycles are way too scary). I listen to bluegrass, Hall & Oates, and some other pretty gay music. I eat dinner at five and go to bed at nine. I enjoy making casseroles for my friends, who call me Grandpa, and papier-mâché puppets for my neighbor's children. I am the opposite of cool.

I haven't worn my Pearl Jam shirt out in public since that day in the grocery store. The humiliation was too great. It's ten years later, but I still can't get rid of it. It mostly hangs around in a drawer. Every now and then I miss it and take it out to wear to bed. When I wake up the next morning, smelling like an old drawer, I wonder if maybe in my dreams somewhere far away I was finally cool.

hotter, more intensive care

I'm reluctant to tell people what I do for a living when I first meet them. I initially try my smart-ass replies, like, "I'm a stunt driver," even though I can barely park my new truck, let alone drive it through flames. Or "I'm a hand model"—as long as I'm modeling something like putting on Chapstick or throwing a softball. Perhaps even "I do all the calligraphy on medical school graduation certificates." I have nice penmanship and there's a lot of calligraphy on those things. I could probably make a fortune.

What I don't want to tell them is the truth, that I'm a nurse. There are a few reasons for this. The first is the dreaded words that generally follow: *Oh, you're a nurse! Can you take a look at this rash and tell me what you think?* No, I will not look at your rash. I don't want to hear about your headaches, your sciatica, or that one time you ate beets and the next morning thought you had to go to the emergency room. Can we just keep our conversation to normal things like tomatoes or smashing the patriarchy?

The second reason I don't like to tell people what I do is because of every sexy nurse picture that exists. Being sexy is what much of society thinks of nurses. If you search the word "nurse" anywhere on the Internet, it's all that shows up: corsets, teddies, heels, fishnet stockings, and little white hats for miles. FYI, we don't wear little white hats anymore. Also, WE DON'T WEAR ANY OF THIS! Hospitals are cold—fishnets wouldn't exactly be practical. And where the fuck are the pockets?

How did this happen?

Let's take a look back at the world's most famous nurse, Florence Nightingale. She was the founder of modern nursing, a hero of the Crimean War who reduced the death rate of her soldier patients from 42 percent to 2 percent. That's impressive work. If you google a picture of Florence, you'll see that she looks stern and impressive, and not at all like she's DTF. In fact, she looks like she could kill you with her bare hands after saving you from a deadly infection. While scowling at you. I bet if Florence Nightingale went to Spirit Halloween in October, she would lose her fucking mind and probably stab Becky the manager over what had become of her once noble profession. How had she gone from hero to whore-o?

According to Thrillist, the problem started way before Florence, as far back as the 1500s, when women with no one to support them had two shitty choices: be a nurse or, better yet, be a prostitute. Or, if you really needed money to do things like eat and survive, do both! Same outfit! Just, please, wash your hands. In the 1700s, New York City passed a law offering convicted prostitutes the option of either jail time or nursing work. The ultimate work-study job!

Flash forward to the 1945 photo of the sailor tongue-kissing— guess who? A nurse!—after we defeated Japan in WWII. This photo, pretty racy for its time, started everyone in the country spanking off to both victory and nurses. Bring on all the nurse pin-ups in photography and the sexy nurses in television and movies. The first television show I ever got aroused to had a nurse slowly unzipping her white uniform. She had on heavy eyeliner and her white hat. I had my hand in my underpants and totally got busted by my mom, who then changed the channel. I forgot about that until I wrote this. Shame on me and shame on mainstream media. According to a study in the *Journal of Advanced Nursing*, 26 percent of the film depictions of nurses between 1990 and 2007 showed them as sex objects. The image has become solidified in our culture and pervades every aspect of the field, though to become a nurse nowadays you actually have to go to school, not just to jail.

I noticed there was something wrong as early as nursing school. For my first clinical rotation, I was told I had to wear a white dress and white hose. I was also expected to carry a cookie sheet around with me to hold supplies on. What the fuck? What other profession requiring a four-year degree starts with a cute little outfit and a cookie sheet? Also, picture me in that getup. Was I going to be a serious professional who could treat illness and perhaps save lives, or somebody's cross-dressing brother delivering sex and perhaps snickerdoodles to those in need? I stomped into my instructor's office in my white flats and started causing trouble. She gave in to pants. With pockets. But she wouldn't budge on the cookie sheet.

I graduated and quickly realized that this attitude of nurses being sex objects was inescapable, even in real life. It was stunning. Early in my ICU career, I was taking care of an older man with heart disease. While I was busy working around him, he said, "If I was twenty years younger, I'd chase you around," with a little click-click and wink-wink. He might've been dealing with his feelings of helplessness and diminished masculinity by attempting to sexualize me, and maybe I should've been a little more compassionate about it, but I wasn't carrying my cookie sheet around anymore and I wasn't having any of his baloney.

I stopped what I was doing, which was basically busting my ass to keep him from dying, and turned to look at him, fuming, and spat, "Go ahead and chase me. I don't run." The look on his face was precious.

I've had a patient tell me he needed me to hold his dick while he peed because his arms suddenly weren't long enough. *No.* I've had patients get up and walk around, then hop into bed and announce that they were ready for their bed baths. *No.* I've had patients ask me if I'd be as sassy on a date as I was at work. *Yes. But not with you.*

I've put up with this shit for twenty-five years, all the while trying to do a good job. I mean, do y'all understand what nurses actually do? If you or a family member has ever been sick enough to need an ICU nurse, then you understand how frustrating this is. We turn ourselves inside out physically, mentally, and emotionally for other people. We are at the beck and call of our patients and their families for twelve hours straight. We miss meals and pee breaks, trying to get by with shoving some stale corn chips in our faces in between doing CPR and holding pressure on a spurting femoral artery. We are not getting rich off of this, by the way. We are certainly not in the mood for your sex bullshit, unless your creepy and inappropriate flirting involves either a hamburger or a shot of tequila—while you are not around.

I've noticed that at my job here in Austin, the nurse-sexing is even worse than normal. I blame this on Texas good ol' boy culture, and also on the fact that I work with some really pretty nurses, who also happen to be badass. But a lot of the patients don't get it. Whenever one of them gets treated inappropriately, say groped or pinched (I swear to God, even now this happens), or if a patient starts talking about his dick a lot or showing it off, or if any inappropriate boner occurs, they automatically sub me in. Surprise, creeper. Have fun flirting with this!

I remember a time when even that didn't work. This old guy, who had been a general in some wars and therefore wanted to be called General, immediately found a way to stroke my leg. Who in the world that isn't attracted to obvious lesbians or incredibly handsome young men wants to stroke my leg? He got this confused look on his face and said, "Is that a girl leg or a boy leg?"

I looked him in the eye and responded, "That's not my leg, General." Problem solved.

And then there is the inappropriate attention my profession garners me outside the hospital. Some of my dates have been just as creepy as my patients. I went out with a girl a few times and when she found out what I did for a living, she started texting me things like, "Hello, NURSE. How about a physical?" *Ew.* I wrote back, "Hello, software engineer. How about you suck my dick instead?" It would be so refreshing if someone offered to suck a nurse's dick. Just a few months ago I sent someone on a dating app a selfie from work. She saw my stethoscope and lost her mind, like maybe I should have it dangling out of my pants instead of hanging around my neck. Am I supposed to fuck her with my stethoscope now? I don't get it. Can't someone just say to me, "You're a nurse? That's impressive. I bet you work really hard to help people. Here's a hamburger and a shot of tequila. May I suck your dick?" Take that, patriarchy.

It should come as no surprise that I'm a big fan of porn. I've seen just about everything that's out there, mostly as "research" for writing these stories. But I've always adamantly refused to watch anything that has to do with nurse porn. It was a rule I had. Well, I'm not very good at following rules. A few years ago, my mom and I had gotten into a fight, and she tried to placate me by sending me a hundred-dollar check for my birthday. I was even more pissed when I got it. I decided the only way I could get back at her was to spend it buying pornography, because the money was already dirty, and because I could be fairly passive-aggressive when it came to my mom. Buying porn with birthday money is the best revenge.

I went to the porn store and something just made me ask where the dirty nurse section was, because I knew there was going to be an entire section for dirty nurses, and there was. I thought, *Let's just see what all the slutty nurse hullabaloo is about*, Mom. The one I bought was called *Nightshift Nurses*. I was intrigued, because it featured HOTTER, MORE INTENSIVE CARE, and also Kayden Kross. I had no idea she went to nursing school, but I was excited to see what she was doing with her degree.

I watched it and discovered that slutty porno nursing is just like regular nursing, so maybe that's why people get confused about us. Porno nurses do all the work while everyone else just sits around. The nurses blew the doctors, rode the patients, and even gave handies to the orderlies. They were busy running around attending to and pleasing everyone, and no one helped. Just like regular nursing.

But you know what? Surprisingly I liked watching that porn. It turned me on to watch those hot women take off their white dresses, throw away their cookie sheets, and put on their gloves to get down like the powerful, taking-care-of-business bitches that nurses really are. I scrolled through to the good parts and whacked off as usual in my office. It turns out that I am just as bad as everyone out there.

So, I'm willing to make a deal. Go ahead, because I know you can't help yourselves, get turned on and spank it to this stuff. Watch TV, go to movies, and ogle all the hot nurses. Keep Becky at Spirit happy by continuing to dress up as a slutty nurse for Halloween—even wear the fucking hat—I don't care. Just do me a favor: don't ever confuse this with real life. Do not come to my hospital or any other and act like an asshole to the nurses; tell your creepy Uncle Bob to knock his shit off too. If you actually can't breathe or are bleeding out, the last thing you want from me is a slutty blow job, and not just because I suck at them. If sex is what you want, do yourself a solid and go visit a librarian.

there are old men in oregon who pump your gas

*T*hey wear dirty coveralls, have rags in their back pockets, and keep dog biscuits in rusty coffee cans. In Oregon everything made of metal is covered in rust, and it's illegal to pump your own gas.

I pulled up to the Texaco in my old Toyota 4x4 that had no radio or air-conditioning, and I rolled the window down by hand to ask the old man to fill it up with unleaded, please. You don't have to say unleaded anymore. We all know there's no more lead. But I was still new to Oregon and clunky at ordering my gas. The old man didn't notice. He just did as I asked, then left me alone in my truck to cry.

Twenty-nine dollars later, he was back at my window just in time to ask me what I was crying about. I broke down and told him all about it. I didn't even manage my pronouns for the outskirts of Oregon. I was new at that too. He didn't care. He just leaned on my window and listened. After my story that old man commanded me out of my Toyota so he could give me a hug and tell me it was all going to be okay. It was foggy-misty out, like it is twenty-three months out of the year in Oregon. It smelled of vinegary pulp from the paper mill, and I had all of my clothes stuffed into three Hefty trash bags in the bed of my truck. Now there was this guy giving me a spectacular hug that made it all seem smaller for a bit.

That night I pulled into a hotel parking lot in Redding, California. I'd been screaming out the truck window for most of the drive to pass the time. When I got to that hotel I was worn out and swollen from all the crying. I walked toward the hotel, carrying nothing, when a woman stopped me to say, "Don't you worry, sweetie. God will take good care of you."

Halfway to the check-in, I woke up from my daze to register what she'd said. Why was she talking to me about God? I made it all the way into the hotel lobby before I realized I had on my Jesus T-shirt. It was Jesus riding on a Harley with giant sunbeams at his back. This woman was trying to be nice to me in a way she thought I would understand. What she didn't see was that the back of my T-shirt said "Nashville Pussy," which is a hard-core rock-and-roll band with a great sense of humor. I didn't have any strong feelings about Jesus, except maybe his image would help to protect me on my journey back to Phoenix after the brutal end of a ten-year relationship, in late May, in a truck with no air-conditioning. It couldn't hurt. I'll mention here that I was wearing another T-shirt under Jesus, and that one was the Beatles, because you can never have too much protection when you're thirty-five years old and all your shit is packed into three Hefty trash bags and you're not sure when or where you'll be able to unpack them.

My ex said she was glad we hadn't lived together in that house in Oregon for very long because it would make it easier for her when I was gone. I was glad I could at least do her that favor after she'd broken my heart and the poem and the ring I'd given to her on a mountaintop for our tenth anniversary. I wished I hadn't lived there long enough to replace the ugly faucet in the kitchen; the new one was beautiful and a complete bitch to install. Now I wished I had that goddamned faucet in one of my pitiful Hefty trash bags. That's what I thought about that night in the hotel in Redding. That, and how complete strangers could sometimes be nicer to me than anyone I'd ever written a poem for.

giddy-up, pilgrim

I was born without my penis. It is a birth defect that has plagued me throughout my entire life. For whatever reason, while I was still in utero, God plucked it from me like a fig and left me with a hole full of confusion where it used to be. I like to imagine me, trying to hold onto it and fight while God reached into my mother and did his will. But tiny baby hands are no defense against a God who knew that I'd need some stories to tell.

For obvious reasons, I spent a great deal of time imagining that I had a penis. I even had dreams about it, perhaps the way someone who's lost his legs dreams about running through a wheat field. In my dreams, my wheat field was full of beautiful girls. And my body, when it was whole, ran amok all over that field and those poor girls. I've been waking myself by humping air ever since I can remember.

As far as I was concerned, I actually had a penis, except physically. My invisible penis was so magical that it got me through sex with boys and girls that wasn't supposed to have anything to do with my penis. I inserted it into situations that didn't even have anything to do with sex, because I was perverted, and good at it.

But all the time I was thinking about and dreaming about this part of me that I wanted so badly, I never once thought about what it might look like. I also never saw it in my dreams, probably because it was always busy being inside of something. So, when a sweet dirty girl took me to the adult store to buy my first replacement penis for sex, I had no idea why I picked the one I did. I honestly didn't put much thought into it besides *That black one looks cool.* Why did I want a black one? I didn't have some deep yearning to be black. I listened to Hall & Oates, for God's sake. But I sure wanted it.

Maybe it's the same as how I really like black cars. Every car I've ever owned has been black. I like how shiny and fast they look when they're clean. So, maybe it's the same thing with the strap-on dicks? To this day, every penis I've had a choice about wearing has been black. An ex once wanted me to buy a Caucasian one. It's not that she wasn't into interracial sex. She was being sweet and thought it'd be a more realistic experience for me. All I could think was, *But then it wouldn't be black.*

The first one I bought, however, was pretty substandard. I guess I wasn't overly concerned about quality, as I didn't yet know how much I'd want to use my new penis, which ended up being a lot. It was cheap, and if you know anything about quality fucking, you know you're going to break that cheap shit at a highly inopportune moment. Even though the girl you're with will mostly be saying "slow down," things will eventually speed up and you'll need to kick it into four-wheel drive. Cheap strap-ons do NOT have four-wheel drive. Even two-wheel drive is iffy. Game over.

I immediately broke that one. The part that held the dildo to the harness ripped off, and I was left with a sideways dangling dick that would make any man wince. The second strap-on I bought was a black thing that was shaped kind of like a penis, but more like an angry nun and strapped onto my thigh. What the fuck? I guess we can blame that on the Lilith Fair. In 1995 Lilith Fair lesbian culture, that was the politically correct type of "sexual attachment pleasure device" to have: one that didn't look like a penis, or even attach where a penis is supposed to go. Because lesbians hated men back then? I dunno.

When this girlfriend and I broke up, I learned the rules about lesbian breakups and strap-ons. Someone gets the dog, someone gets the camping equipment, and no one gets the dick. Poor little nun. She got thrown away along with the Sarah McLachlan albums you bought together in an act of "sacred cleansing." In other words, this shit gets expensive.

Then I moved to San Francisco, on a travel nurse assignment for three months. A week after moving there I started having sex with my boss, because that's a really good idea. If you'd seen her, you would've wanted me to fuck her. She was a Pisces, which meant she was the good kind of dirty. She could sense immediately that I was born to fuck with a strap-on (mostly because I told her). She told me about a store named "Good Vibrations" and something called the "Feeldoe," which is a dildo that has a knobby thing attached that goes into your vagina and holds it in place. This way, you don't need to strap it on, there isn't all the hurried buckling and fumbling, and it looks more realistic without the harness. It's just there being awesome.

When I went to get one, I was disappointed to learn that they didn't come in black, just bright blue or bright purple. I wondered how realistic that would look. I would never drive a bright blue or purple car. I bought the purple one because the blue one was just too big, even for a Pisces. It was weird putting it up in there. I'm not used to putting anything except the normal everyday things into my vagina, and the knobby part of this thing was really big in order to hold it in. It turned out that putting this on was even more awkward than putting on a harness. I finally got it stuck up there, and my Feeldoe was ready for action.

When my boss and I started at it, though, things got weird. The whole time I was fucking her, doing a good job, listening to her awesome Pisces sex noises, the Feeldoe was wiggling inside of my vagina. So I had to feel and think about my vagina. It was like going to a really great party where everyone is drinking and dancing and making out and you realize your mom is sitting in the corner watching. If I'm fucking you with my penis, even if it's bright purple, I don't want my vagina at that party, thanks.

When I left San Francisco I left my boss but I didn't leave my Feeldoe, because that relationship wasn't about love, it was about her red hair and getting a good work schedule. While I didn't really care so much for this toy, it was expensive and I was tired of throwing shit away. I packed it up in a box with a bunch of my other stuff and mailed it back home so I wouldn't have to smuggle my bright purple vagina-dick onto the plane. I got a call five days later from the friend I sent my stuff to, saying that a hole had been ripped in the corner of the box en route, and when it arrived at her door, my bright purple vagina-dick was sticking out of it. I like to imagine the FedEx guy using it as a handle.

The next time I went shopping for a penis replacement, I spared no expense. I had learned some lessons and was tired of being disappointed. This was my dick, after all. I was finally going to have exactly what I wanted. What I bought was called "The Jaguar," and that made me quite happy. It was an expensive, shiny black penis housed in a high-end leather harness with chrome buckles.

The leather smelled amazing coming out of the package. The first time I put it on, it felt like I was putting on a really great motorcycle jacket and I was going to go for a great ride. This setup was an unstoppable pair. When I wore it I didn't think about my vagina at all. And when I kicked it into four-wheel drive, the leather kept up and made that great creaking sound and nothing broke. My dick was sleek and sturdy and classic, perhaps like me, if I was also black and didn't still listen to Hall & Oates.

I've had this harness ever since. It's been many years and I've stopped throwing away my dick after failed love affairs, because it's mine. And it's awesome. It will never break, and I know it so well that all the usual fumbling and buckling of getting a boner isn't an issue. Because it's The Jaguar!

Here's where I need to talk to men about how nice and easy they have it. Guys, you get excited, you get a boner, you're not in fifth-grade math class anymore and you're ready to go. You don't have to put anything on except maybe a condom. When I want to be inside of a girl with my dick, I have to plan and be well coordinated. I need to make sure she's okay with using a strap-on. It's usually implied that a guy will have a boner during sex, but I have to ask. Also, I have to make sure I've run the dishwasher recently, because no one ever got laid by saying, "Here, let me wash this first."

And while it's a complete turn-on to fuck with my strap-on, let's be honest: it's not the same as if it were an actual dick. While I can make a woman come with it, I can't really feel it, except in my brain, which lucky for me does a great job of translating it to the rest of my body. With the right amount of concentration and pressure in the right places, I can totally get off. But I can't tell if it slips out. I'm sure dicks slip out all the time, right? Shit gets all crazy down there, but I have to be told that I need to stick it back in. Awesome.

And even though I'm pretty good at putting on The Jaguar by now, things will have to stop while I do. FYI, once it's on I may have to get up and walk around for a minute, maybe go get a beer from the refrigerator, because I just like the way that looks and feels, okay? I'm about to run through your wheat field. Give me a minute to get used to my legs.

Then, everything is awesome. My imagined penis magically gets to exist in the world, it magically works the way I want it to, and I'm not even dreaming. Sometimes, it's even as good as my dreams are. Like the time I had sex with a girl when she was covered in gold glitter, because I am very, very lucky. When we were done I looked down at The Jaguar and it too was covered in glitter. I stared at it shimmering in the near-darkness and thought, *I AM A UNICORN!* When I picked it up off the floor and put it in the dishwasher the next day, I was sad. Though I needn't have been sad, because the universal truth about glitter is correct. It never really goes away.

Then, there was the time I was driving back from a date I'd had in the country. I'd spent the afternoon with a beautiful woman in the middle of nowhere, getting incredibly sweaty while scorpions skittered across the floor and cows watched me through the windows. It was a day like John Wayne might've had. *Giddy-up, Pilgrim.* It only got better when, on the way home, I realized that I had both my black strap-on and a black gun in my black car with me. What I thought, besides how cool my life is, was what if I went to Red's Indoor Gun Range on the way home? What if instead of the gun, I took my strap-on in, slapped it on the counter, and said, "I'd like to buy some live rounds for this thing, because this fucker's been shooting blanks for years."

Don't worry. I just drove home and loaded the dishwasher.

the wonder
of migration

/ moved to Texas in 2006. It was February, and I was surprised
at how cold it could be in Austin. The first night in my rental
house was spent on the floor, as my furniture hadn't yet arrived.
The dog and the cat were suddenly affectionate that night, curling
up on top of me and even into each other to stay warm.

If you'd asked me at any time in my life where I wanted to live,
I never once would have said Texas. To me, Texas was just a place
that made bad presidents, big hair, and highways that didn't end.
But then I had a special dream.

One night, probably in 2001 or 2002, I had a dream about a
giant white billboard on top of a building. In big red letters on that
billboard was the word "Austin." I woke up in my bed in Phoenix
and knew it meant something. I told my girlfriend about it and that
it was important. Her reply to me was, "I'm never setting foot in
Texas. There's nothing good there." Case closed. But the truth was,
I never forgot that dream and that important dream hangover-y
feeling.

Fast-forward a few years to when Stacey and I broke up. We
had spent most of our relationship together in Phoenix where we
both grew up, but we'd recently moved to Oregon for her new job.

After the breakup I moved back to Phoenix but quickly realized that I hated it there. Or I guess I was tired of who I was there. We had been together for ten years, and we'd spent that time buying, living in, fixing up, and then selling houses in just about every part of that city. We had worked together in just about every hospital. There was nowhere I could go in that town to get away from the last ten years and the ghost of her. I needed to leave.

To get out of there as soon as possible, I took a travel nurse assignment in San Francisco. I didn't decide to go there because I was a newly single lesbian/transy dude and that's exactly where you should go if you find yourself in a similar situation, though it did work out nicely. It was just the first thing available. Being a nurse is a great career if you want to get the fuck out of somewhere, STAT.

When that assignment ended, I was ready for something new and more permanent. I was ready to go toward something instead of running away from something. That's when I thought of the dream I'd had years ago, and I just knew I had to go. In one of those beautiful fuck-it moments, I packed my shit and moved to Austin. The minute I pulled in to this town, I knew I was home. My ex was so wrong about Texas.

There are weird things about living here, like the language. "Y'all" is a thing here. So is "all y'all," which is the plural of "y'all." It seems Texans don't consider the multitude that "all" can indicate. Whatever.

Then there's the Texas pride thing. Everything in Texas seems to be an advertisement for the state of Texas. Texas T-shirts, hats, bumper stickers, tattoos, beer koozies, yard signs, jewelry, corn chips, etc., are everywhere. A large number of folks here have the word "Texas" tattooed on themselves. Sometimes I want to scream, "But all y'all are already in Texas!"

In the break room at my job in Texas someone had left a cheese plate, which is the most unusual thing I'd ever seen in a hospital break room. The thing about this cheese plate, however, was there was a giant block of cheddar in the middle of it and it was carved in the shape of Texas. I'm pretty sure I'll never go to New Hampshire and find cheese carved in the shape of New Hampshire. I wouldn't even know what the shape of New Hampshire is.

Another weird thing about Texas is the political atmosphere surrounding sex. Not too long ago dildos were illegal here. As I couldn't buy one at any stores, I had to get on the Internet to find them, where, ironically, they were all named after Texas culture. There was the Lonestar, the Outlaw, the Bandit, the Spur, and my favorite, the Rodeo Rick (see: Rick Perry, once governor of Texas).

So you could have a machine gun here, no problem. But if you walked into a convenience store with Rodeo Rick strapped to your belt, you're going to jail. I reckon they're afraid you'd stroll into the 7-Eleven armed as such and say, "Give me all the cash you've got in the register or you're going eight seconds with the Governor."

They've since changed this law and it's now legal to buy a dildo here, but for a while they needed to be referred to as "educational models" (insert all the jokes here). The only stipulation was that you couldn't own more than six "educational models." Maybe because they didn't want anyone to open up a school. I don't know.

Now, though, no one cares about the dildos, perhaps because one or more of our state politicians may or may not have been caught with one up their ass. So, good news: if dildos are your thing, you can now come to Texas and pick up one (or six).

Ladybugs are migratory. They go places on their tiny little wings, traveling and arriving and unpacking and staying for brief periods, then traveling off again in time to keep their schedules of departures and reservations.

I found this out the hard way. Not that anything about ladybugs could really ever be hard. A number of springs ago, I planted a wall of sunflowers in one of my yards in Phoenix that managed to attract a herd of insects that wanted to eat them. Not cool, herd. I went to the nursery for help, and they sold me a cup of ladybugs that I was to spread on my flowers. Ladybugs are not only migratory but also carnivorous, and they like to eat the bad guys.

The sticker on the cup said it contained three hundred ladybugs. I peered in at them crawling around on what looked to be an old paper towel and could barely fathom that there were three hundred in there. I had a small ladybug village in a paper cup. Were they related? Did they all hatch from the same parents? Did they like each other? I drove them home carefully lodged in the cup holder and released them over my fledgling sunflowers. They all flew away. Gone. Immediately. Not one stopped to roost on my flowers, not one hesitated to eat a bug for the road. They all just flew away in a cloud of orange as I stood in my yard and yelled at them to come back.

Shortly after I arrived in Austin, as the cold of February gave way to the pleasantness that is March here, those damned ladybugs showed up again. That's right: Austin, Texas, is apparently on their migratory path. It may even be a major hub for them, who knows? But I can tell you that all three hundred that I had let go in Phoenix moved into the guest room of my rental house in Austin.

I obviously couldn't confirm that they were all the same ones. They moved too quickly to get a good look at all of them. But with some there was a definite familiarity, a knowing that passed between us when we looked at each other. I could tell they were ashamed. I had purchased them, brought them home and set them free, and they left me standing there in my yard with my hands in my pockets. I bet they thought they'd never see me again. Now that I was here I bet they wished they'd treated me with a bit of respect, maybe eaten a bug or two before leaving just so they didn't seem rude.

They only came out during the day and would cover the same sunny corner every time, a mass of moving little orange speckled things. I had no idea where they went at night, but when it got dark, they would disappear. Maybe they went over to a neighbor's house where they had little bunkbeds or sleeping bags.

This lasted for about a month, and then, just as quickly as they appeared, they were gone. Off to some other hub on their migratory path.

I told my dad about them. His response was, "You need to call an exterminator. It's just like any other infestation."

No, it's not, Dad. It's magical. Plus, what kind of dick kills a ladybug on purpose?

I did some research into the symbolism surrounding ladybugs. The only thing I could find was that they are associated with good luck. I moved my writing desk into that sunny corner of the guest room and thought about those ladybugs every time I turned on my computer while I lived in that house. Sure, they were rude to me once, but maybe they'd be good to me from now on.

when
alligators
attack

*T*he human body opens to the outside world in nine or ten places. It's overwhelming to consider how vulnerable this makes us to the sheer number of things that are wafting into and out of us daily. I used to work in an emergency room, and I can report that the number of things that waft into people accidentally while they are in the shower alone is staggering. Apparently, people slip and fall upon random things like shampoo bottles or pepper mills frequently while bathing. My favorite, though, was the Ken doll that accidentally slipped into someone's rectum and had to be removed by a doctor wielding forceps. It was a breach delivery, but I digress. What I mean to tell you about is something completely different.

Many Saturdays ago, after a decent night of drinking and watching the musical *Xanadu*, I was startled awake at 1 a.m. by the feeling of something crawling into my right ear. That's not a pleasant sensation, waking up from a beer-induced slumber to the sound and feeling of tiny, crunchy leglets navigating your interior. Whatever it was crawled and crawled and crawled. Bad enough, I thought. But then, when it got in good and deep, it began biting my eardrum, which hurt worse than the *Xanadu* roller-skate disco music I'd subjected myself to earlier in the evening.

I've told you I'm a nurse, and over the years I've learned to remain calm in intense or even scary situations. Well, I didn't really pull that off here. I shot out of bed naked, screaming, "GET OUT, GET OUT, GET OUT!" while jumping up and down on one leg and crying. This was obviously one of the finer moments of my life. Too bad no one was there to witness it.

You know what's worse than the searing pain of being bitten repeatedly on the eardrum? Hearing it. Way the fuck up close: *chewchewchewchew.* It would stop for a second, then I'd feel it slither or stroll or line dance around in there, then it would start the chewing on me business again, and I'd start jumping around and crying and trying to scream it out of my ear. Is there a hidden camera in my house?

In my rational state, I decided the only thing I could do was to drive to my hospital for help. In between the crawling/chewing/screaming/jumping, I pulled some clothes on and got into the car and tore off and blew through every goddamned red light while still screaming and crying from the pain and the terror of it all, daring any cop to pull me over and try to figure out how much K2 I'd ingested. There was a moment on Loop 360 when I thought, *Well, at least I'll get a good story out of this, and it could only be better if I also had diarrhea.* Right after that thought, before I made the final turn onto the road that led to the hospital where I would certainly humiliate myself with my psychotic behavior in front of my coworkers, ~~I had diarrhea~~ I felt that fucker crawl out of my ear.

Have you ever seen anyone try to get away from themselves while attempting to stay in the driver's seat and still actually operate a car? I knew it was out, but I didn't know where it went; it was dark and I was looking mostly at the road. All I knew to do was to perpetrate the most violent assault on myself—my shoulder, my arm, my head and hair—to make sure that thing was either dead or scared enough of me to stay the fuck away.

I turned around and drove home, steering with my knee so I could keep my hands over my ears. When I got home I tore all the sheets and pillows off the bed and took off my clothes. Then I drank a large glass of wine, stuffed earplugs into both sides, and went back to sleep like it was just another Saturday night, because that's how it was around my house for a while. It was all just bizarre enough that the next morning I wondered if perhaps I'd imagined it or dreamed it. But my eardrum throbbed like someone had raped the side of my head with an alligator.

I called a friend and told her about it, and she said, "Why didn't you just pour rubbing alcohol into your ear? It would have crawled right out." She said it like everyone knows this. Like everyone in a state of complete panic and terror would walk into the bathroom, open the cabinet, and handle the situation. Thanks a lot, friend, but I wasn't really scraping great thoughts together at 1 a.m. on a drunken Saturday night with an alligator in my ear.

And as I haven't owned rubbing alcohol since I got my ears pierced in the sixth grade, I went the next day to buy the biggest bottle of rubbing alcohol available. I got a ride to Walgreens from my friend, though, because there's only so much driving you can do with your knee.

the simple comfort of rocks and underpants

(just one more horrifying event)

*M*y dog and I were once attacked by a pit bull. I'd say that my dog and I were attacked by another dog, but nothing about this pit bull reminded me of any other dog I'd seen.

I'd just finished a day of hot and sweaty yard work. I wasn't wearing underpants because I had on loose jeans and saw it as an opportunity to let everything breathe, even the parts of me that don't have lungs. Commando in the yard is my choice every time.

My friend Robin was coming over for a steak dinner, so my plan was to walk to the Texaco at the end of the street and buy some beer to go with dinner. And probably a few to have before the dinner on my porch before I put on underwear. More of the breathing process.

I walked with my dog (a severely loyal rat terrier) down the street, but we never made it to the Texaco. A hundred feet from the store, a pit bull punched his square head through the wooden fence that was supposed to keep him enclosed. He grabbed my dog by the face and began pulling him into his yard, presumably to eat him.

I was as loyal to this dog as he was to me. He accompanied me everywhere. He didn't need a leash; he just hung out alongside me being a cool-as-shit dog. Now here he was, my loyal companion, being dragged into the lair of a pit bull.

Some primal part of my brain took over. I grabbed the back end of my dog while the pit bull had him by the face, and I tried to pull him back out through the fence. I yelled, "Fuck off! Fuck off! Fuck off!" Aside from the screaming, that's the only thing that would come out of my mouth. The pit bull wouldn't let go and kept pumping itself backwards, trying to muscle my dog free from my grasp and into his yard.

I was screaming, and my dog was bleeding and pooping all over me. I, at one point, reached into the pit bull's mouth with my left hand to try to pry open his jaw. Don't ever do that. For starters, it won't work. That jaw is clamped down harder than a vise. Also, there are teeth in that mouth, and they will try to eat your hand. The pit bull managed to bite my fingers while simultaneously pulling my dog in by the face. Tricky move, pit bull.

I couldn't tell you how long this went on. I don't know what besides panic was going on in my head when I saw a rock the size of a fist on the ground next to the fence. Somehow, without knowing what I was doing, I picked up this rock and was able to put my hand through the hole in the fence while still holding on to my dog with a bloody hand and arm and started bashing this asshole of a pit bull in the head with the rock. I bashed it over and over, and distinctly remember two thoughts penetrating the terror while I was doing it: 1) *Well, shit. Robin won't be able to come over for steaks now because I'm going to have to take my bloody hand and my dog to the hospital when this is over.* And 2) *Oh my God, I don't have on any underpants.* That's what my brain chose to do while I was beating this dog in the head with a rock.

Somehow, I managed to beat that pit bull through the fence

hard enough that he finally let go of my dog. We both ran bleeding and crying back to my house while neighbors stood watching us wide-eyed. I made some quick phone calls, all with my bloody hand clenched into a fist, because I was afraid to open it and see that maybe my fingers were hanging by bones or tendons—I couldn't be sure—there was just so much blood. My pants were covered in my dog's crisis poop, I didn't have on any underwear, and I'd have to go to the hospital where I work because that's how my health insurance works. It works on humiliation.

I decided that priority number one while we were waiting for rides to the hospital and the emergency vet clinic was to put on underpants, because I am the dumbest person to ever exist on the planet. Do you know how hard it is, when you're sweating and bleeding and crying and can only use one hand, to take off your pants, put on clean underpants, and then pull a different pair of pants back on? And why? Sure, I've got some wounds to deal with. On my hand. Do I think the ER staff is going to whisk me back to exam room one, take one look at my hand, and decide that it's time for an emergency pap smear? Have I told you I'm an ICU nurse?

But I was committed to the underpants. I also put on fresh deodorant because I was going to see people I know. *You're welcome, ER staff.*

I got eight stitches in my hand that was otherwise fine. My dog had surgery and was somehow fine. I went back the next day and picked up that pit bull-head-beating rock, because I wanted that fucking rock. I still have that rock, and when people mess with me, I like to say, "Don't make me get my fucking rock." That scares them into behaving. I called a lawyer because the owner of the pit bull wouldn't take any responsibility for what his dog did. In fact, he went so far as to tell me how sweet his dog was. I sued his ass and he moved away with his sweet little pit bull, hopefully to somewhere with a cinderblock fence and no little dogs or, God forbid, children running around.

I know I'm going to get a bunch of flak from people telling me how pit bulls have gotten a bad rap because of the behavior of a few dogs. Whatever. I don't care. I kneeled on the ground, a rat terrier's length away from the eyes and mouth of one of those dogs, and I can tell you that I've never seen anything as possessed by violence and intent on doing harm. That pit bull wanted to kill and eat my dog and didn't care if I was trying to stand in his way.

It took me a long time before I could close my eyes without seeing that dog in my head. Even now, I can't stand to be around any large dog that's not on a leash, because I go right back to that day and that fence. What I'm saying is watch out for pit bulls. And it's a good idea to always be wearing underpants. You never know when you'll be taking a surprise trip to the emergency room.

treasure hunt

/ live in an interesting neighborhood. It's like there's some sort of cultural experiment happening daily. There are elderly homeowners who don't wear enough clothing while watering their enormous front lawns to excess with a hose, there are new home-owners with their Democrat bumper stickers and plastic baby toys cluttering their front yards, and there are a bunch of other folks who seemingly don't care about anything and like to throw shit in my front yard as they drive/walk by, and entertain themselves late at night by playing mailbox baseball (see: good, clean fun circa 1975).

There's a Texaco at the end of my street. That's a red flag to look for when purchasing real estate, but I was blinded by the sheer number of porches on my house. Deciding which one to sit on and drink Busch Light tallboys is on my "Excellent Problems to Have" list. They've also added a taco truck at the corner with the Texaco. Beer and tacos at the end of my street? Imagine the traffic! Imagine the trash in my yard, because who could possibly bear to hang onto a taco wrapper or an empty can of whatever until one reaches a trash receptacle? No one should be expected to drive with this shit in a car. This is America, for fuck's sake! With the crack of a win-dow and a casual flip of the wrist, into my yard it goes.

I like to play a game I call Treasure Hunt, where I go out into my front yard on Sunday mornings and look for new stuff. Sunday mornings are never a disappointment.

The following is a list of items I've found lying in my front yard:

- My mailbox (for the fifth time, goddammit)
- Jägermeister bottle (empty)
- Condom (used)
- Tampon (used)
- Rearview mirror (driver's side)
- Thong underwear (TREASURE!)

Ok, so condoms and Jäger bottles I can kind of understand. And maybe, if I stretch my imagination a bit, I can see how the tampon might go along with the used condom (don't make me do the math for you). But the thong underwear? Aren't they expensive? Do the ladies drive by my house and become so sexually aroused by my awesomeness that they can't stand it and need to fling their underclothes into my yard? I'm choosing to believe this.

This morning the only thing I found was half of a bird shell. It looks like even the birds are like, "Fuck it. Just throw it in Holly's yard."

I'm going to get a taco.

i never said
i was good
at behavior

I't's best if you're hungry. Beer on a full stomach is underwhelming at best. But when you're empty in there and the sun is shining at three-quarters day, it's like God himself comes through the radio to announce, "Pull over and buy yourself a cold tallboy, Holly." That's why he makes long and winding roads that drift through the beautiful Texas Hill Country.

I go into the Short Stop or the Friendly Mart, and there they are, in enormous open bins in the middle of the store. Lying together. Stacked perfectly against each other, one after glorious one. The shiny cans I love are bathed in a mountain of ice, begging me to take them home like dogs at the pound.

This is just another strange thing about Texas. In Arizona we didn't have these open beer bins suggesting that, although it's illegal, why not take one for the road, cowboy? If you wanted a single in Arizona you had to actually open the cooler door (*gasp*) and break a six-pack. Such behavior says, "I'm tearing apart the natural order of the regular beer drinker, the one who buys the whole six-pack and waits until she gets home to drink it." If you break the rings, you aren't waiting and you've breached all manner of civility. Go ahead and just throw litter out of your car while you're at it (especially if you're driving by my yard).

But here in Texas no one cares about this silly stuff. Mavericks are celebrated. At my favorite convenience store they sell single tallboys, giant hunting knives, and miniature glass figurines. *You take your pick, Maverick.*

When I take my tallboy to the counter, they ask if I want Daisy Dukes or Hip Hops. Daisy Dukes are the tiny brown bags that barely cover the whole beer, and Hip Hops are the big bags that hang all up and down your beer's ass. I'm a Daisy Dukes girl: I like the classy look of a brown paper bag but don't want a mouthful of it with my beer. Plus, Daisy Duke.

I plunk down my $1.83 and I'm out the door, following God's orders on my way to a dinner party in Dripping Springs or the junk stores in Llano. God stops talking through the radio, and country music spills out of it instead. I lift my beer to my mouth when no other cars are around or even when other cars are around if I'm feeling particularly dangerous. I sing to the music and feel the beer tingle in my empty stomach and flow down into my legs, happy about simple good times and my shitty taste in beer.

good morning, peacocks!

 walk down the stairs, through the hall, and into the kitchen, and the blue wallpaper peacocks tell me good morning in bright cheery voices. I think, *Good morning, peacocks!* and take my place at the table with my brother and sister. We are all rubbing our eyes and shifting in our chairs as quietly as possible because we can feel the familiarity of another bad morning. It's January and cold in that Omaha kitchen. My mom has all the burners of the stove on to heat the room, and they rage electric orange. She bends over and lights a cigarette on one and turns on the radio without saying a word to us.

The room smells like cinnamon, and it almost makes the chill sting a bit less. Cinnamon toast is a thing my mom can accomplish in the morning.

We eat and the radio DJ announces a contest. Answer the question, "What lady has the biggest mouth in America?" My mom is bleary-eyed and barely awake after her late night waiting tables at the restaurant. She has three ungrateful kids, a husband who unwittingly stole her away from her childhood dreams, and only four coils of heat and a cigarette to keep it all together. But I know she's smart. I see her stacks of library books lying around the house.

I hear her say words like "magnanimous," which I had to look up in the dictionary last week. I look up her words all the time.

I see in her eyes that she knows the answer to the DJ's question. I know it too, because I'm also smart. I say out loud, "The Statue of Liberty!"

My mom surprises us all and calls the radio station. She never does anything like this. This is fun and exciting! Despite the incredible handicap of a rotary dial she makes it through. When the DJ picks up and tells her she's on the air and does she know the answer, she looks at me and says, "The Statue of Liberty," even though I can tell by her voice and the way she's looking at me that she knows it's wrong. The correct answer is the Mississippi River.

My brother and sister are ready to throw their toast at me because I just lost the contest for us. I don't care. My mom picked me that morning over the unhappiness that was drowning her every day. The peacocks would be excited for me.

following your dreams while avoiding acorns

My mom broke my leg, and I'm pretty sure it was on purpose. She and I hadn't talked for a while. It was seven months since she'd died, and things had been silent between us. I expected her to show up somehow and say something important to me or tell me she was thinking about me or even that she was sorry about some stuff, but I got nothing. To be fair, I hadn't tried to talk to her, either. I guess the best relationship we could have after her death was a quiet one. There was a novel peace about it. At the age of forty-six, I was finally able to have some peace with my mother. I don't know what possessed me to suddenly speak to her.

"Please, Mom. Please help me." It was a beautiful morning on a romantic beach weekend with my girlfriend. We'd gotten up early and gone for a run. My girlfriend was still running because she didn't need to stop and wheeze after a half mile like I did. I sat in the sand and watched her tiny athletic body continuing down the beach before turning my gaze to the ocean before me. I felt calm and happy and lucky to have the life that I had. It was the nicest feeling. I sent up a little gratitude prayer for all of it, and then I decided it was the time to talk to my mom. What came out of me was a plea for help. I didn't plan that.

I'd known for a long time that I wanted to put this book together, but for whatever reason (procrastination, fear of failure, fear of success, floor needed sweeping, roof needed shingling, cat needed training—you pick one), I was having trouble sitting down and actually doing it. When I finally thought to speak to my mother, I asked her for some help with it.

It was odd because my mom hadn't ever been interested in my writing. I'd try to tell her about it and she would say something like, "What? I'm a little busy with my ironing," or "Did you hear that Uncle So-and-So has a new tumor?" It wasn't her idea of fun, having a daughter who wrote about awkward sex and crushes on girls. She wanted only to hear about how I was writing the Great American Novel. I finally quit trying to talk to her about it until she was dead and I was sitting alone on a beach looking at the ocean.

I sent that plea to her out into the morning sky, and immediately three pelicans flew into my line of vision, flapped once in unison, and carried my message across the Great Whatever to where my mom was so she could hear it. I was sure of it. I got up and walked back to the hotel, and when my girlfriend got back from her six-mile run, I told her that I'd just talked to my mom for the first time. She said, "Great. I'm hungry. Let's go to Joe's Crab Shack and then the water park." Pure romance.

No one got hurt at Joe's Crab Shack, but five minutes after I got to the water park, someone came down a slide behind me and cracked me hard in the right leg. I knew something serious was wrong, but instead of going directly to the first aid office I walked to the lazy river for a little relaxing float with my broken leg, which was starting to look pretty bad. I tried to be lazy as hell on that river while teenagers floated by giggling and flirting with each other (*Nothing to see here, kids, except this weirdo floating in the river with a giant purple leg*), but after five minutes I discovered that this was the one time that floating down a river on an inner tube didn't make everything better for me. My girlfriend did her best to be gentle yanking me up and out of my tube when the pain became too much. Then I walked on my broken leg to the first aid office, because water parks are not for sissies. When they showed me my broken leg on the X-ray at the urgent care, all I could think was, *Holy shit, I asked my mom for help and she busted my fucking leg! On the first ride!*

Nothing will kill a romantic beach weekend faster than breaking your leg. In fact, nothing will kill feeling lucky to have the life you have faster than breaking your leg.

I suddenly couldn't walk, work, or drive, and everything became difficult. Bathing was difficult. Getting dressed was difficult. Cooking, which I liked even more than walking, was difficult. And sex? My girlfriend was allergic to the giant fiberglass cast on my leg. Not that sex for us involved me ever putting my leg anywhere intimate, but I'd run the risk of brushing it against her if we even tried. So, cross sex off the list too, and then just go ahead and kill me.

What was easy to do with a broken leg was taking pain pills and drinking, which I managed to do at breakneck pace. I became a helpless, pitiful, miserable mess. You really haven't lived until you pee yourself in the middle of the night because you're so drunk and stoned that you can't figure out how to ride your stupid knee scooter to the bathroom in time. *Really, Mom? This is how you help me?*

I'd gone from being a healthy, independent, active, hardworking, youthful, middle-aged handsome adult to being stuck in a chair in my house with my leg elevated and a bunch of clothes strewn around me that smelled like pee. My girlfriend, clearly the luckiest person on earth, would still kiss me and tell me she loved me before going off to work, or to run twenty-five miles, or to get her pretty hair done while I sat on my ass and wallowed and ate Doritos (Nacho Cheese. Never Cool Ranch).

After two weeks of this, of behaving like a spoiled little child who doesn't get what she wants and is a little disgusting, I woke up and got my shit together, because it's not like I had cancer, or was paralyzed for life, or even had an STD. I just had a broken leg. But if I didn't get it together, I'd very quickly also be a single, drunken, bitter, middle-aged handsome adult who is addicted to pain pills and has to wear a diaper to bed. As great as that sounded, I went ahead and made a different choice.

I threw out all my pills and my Doritos and started bathing regularly. I wasn't going to give up beer, because who am I to be that drastic? But I at least cut out the tequila, vodka, and whiskey. Maybe I couldn't run or drive or even walk, but what I could do, when I wasn't drunk or stoned, was scoot. I got on my little knee scooter and started rolling hard-core. I was so sick of being dependent and cooped up in the house that I started knee-scooting everywhere. It's amazing how far you can get on one of those things if you're dedicated and have nothing else to do.

There's a coffee shop about a mile from my house, and I scooted there just about every day for exercise and to kill the boredom. On the way I sang to my new Indigo Girls album while memorizing where all the jacked-up sidewalk cracks, overgrown bushes, and speed bumps were. I could tell which neighbor had had a great night by who had an extra car parked in the driveway in the morning that blocked my sidewalk. After about a week of just sitting around at the coffee shop, I decided I might as well start putting this book together. What else did I have to do?

My mom wasn't being a jerk when she broke my leg. She wasn't blowing me off or trying to change the subject or hurt me on purpose. She waited until I was ready to ask her, and then she forced me to sit down and do this thing that has been my dream since I can remember. With one crack of my fibula, she handed me the time and the space to finally do what I needed to do. Go figure.

My neighbors thought I was a little odd, but I didn't care. They honked and waved at me while I sang and scooty-scooted up and down the streets for three months, sometimes with a beer in my basket, enjoying the weather while doing my best to watch out for acorns, which will wipe you out and land you on your ass faster than you can say "Fuck you, acorns." Hey neighbors, why don't you sweep your goddamned sidewalks once in a while? I have places to scoot and shit to write, and I already have one broken leg.

interesting things i learned when i broke my leg

- Crutches will fall no matter where you put them.
- I shouldn't have bought the house with the gravel driveway.
- Turning a vacuum on and off is a thing meant for someone with two working legs.
- Why am I trying to vacuum? Didn't I break my leg?
- Along with acorns, my Chihuahua's stuffed toy Gnomio can fuck things up in a hurry.
- Everyone was quite nice and helpful to me after I broke my leg. Everyone except my girlfriend, who still wanted me to vacuum.
- You can get a peg leg thing that straps onto your knee so you can kind of walk and sweep the floor. It's not vacuuming, but it will get your girlfriend off your back.
- Going to the bathroom independently, making dinner, carrying my own beer, and putting on pants are things I will never again take for granted.
- Taking an online calligraphy class is not an adequate substitute for having a meaningful work life.

- Listening to Hall & Oates while practicing calligraphy makes me really happy, but I shouldn't post about it on Facebook.
- There are lots of people who sit at the coffee shop for long periods of time every single day, seemingly doing nothing. Not many of them have broken legs.
- I had time to do all kinds of interesting things, like get cast in online videos where I'm sitting and talking about frozen peas, write silly articles for the work newsletter titled "Hello from My Chair," and send Dave Grohl a Facebook message asking if I can join the Foo Fighters on his broken leg tour. He didn't write back.
- I love driving around in my car and dancing to music not meant for my generation. The first day I could drive again, I turned on the radio and experienced unexpectedly joyful immaturity while listening to fresh beats. Being an adult is overrated.

Photo by: Holly Lorka

Beans and Gnomio

halloween
and i are not
great friends

I 've never been good at Halloween. I blame it on that time in kindergarten when my mom dressed me as a cowgirl and pissed me off. Or the year when all I wanted to be was Dracula because I had a natural widow's peak but no actual Dracula costume. I came up with an elaborate idea to steal my sister's red denim skirt and snap it around my neck as the cape and then put an entire jar of Vaseline in my hair to slick it back into place. I had no fangs, no white face makeup, and no drawn-on pointy eyebrows. Basically, absolutely nothing about me said Dracula except what was in my heart. When I showed up at people's doors that year, they probably thought I was some sorry kid with a skirt around my neck and really greasy hair saying, "Trick or treat." *Okay, kid, whatever the fuck you are. Here's your Tootsie Roll. Let me know if you need help opening it.*

Maybe you already know this, but Vaseline doesn't wash out of your hair with shampoo. The next night my mom had my head under the tub faucet with a bottle of vinegar, which was her answer to everything. She used a lot of hot water and vinegar and made my head sore, but she couldn't get all the Vaseline out. I went to school with greasy hair that smelled like vinegar for a long time. Fuck you, Halloween.

2015, of course, was no different. My leg was broken, but I'd adapted to my new life on a scooter. Halloween morning I woke up feeling good. It was a beautiful day, and I had fun plans to go to a neighborhood party that night. All I needed was to have my girlfriend drive me to Michael's for last-minute costume details. I allowed myself to get excited to dress up!

I should've smelled the vinegar coming.

I woke up early, but my girlfriend was still sleeping, so I scooted it over to the coffee shop and worked for a while. When she woke up, she offered to come pick me up after she ran eighty-five miles. I was hungry, so I scooted to the little bistro next to the coffee shop for lunch. I'd eaten there a million times, and it was usually quite delicious and otherwise uneventful.

I started feeling ill soon after eating, before she came to get me. I was stuck there on my scooter, and I developed a large case of the struggles. I was feeling too sick to push for home, feeling too sick to do anything but scoot outside and wait for her. I was frustrated by my dependence. I couldn't just get in my car and drive home to barf or lie down or whatever I needed to do. I had to wait for someone to help me. So, on top of not feeling well, I got upset and started to cry on my scooter in the parking lot. It was the saddest thing ever.

When she arrived, I hopped into the car while she tossed my scooter in the back and the struggles overwhelmed me. I bawled. I was sick, frustrated, and tired. My body hurt, I hated having to scoot and bum rides from people, and I was on the verge of throwing up. I decided I still had to go to Michael's, though, because I needed to work on my Halloween costume.

We weren't even halfway there when I puked in her car. To my credit, I had the foresight to grab one of her reusable shopping bags out of the back seat to throw up into. Not to my credit, it was her favorite reusable shopping bag, the one with the pineapple and clipper ship on it, and the one with the giant hole in the bottom. I sat there in the passenger seat puking and crying while puke dripped out the bottom of the bag onto my pants and her car. She hurriedly pulled over and grabbed the bag from me and handed me a cooler to throw up into instead of her favorite bag (Who has a favorite reusable bag, anyway?).

She dumped out my puke while I sat there in the front seat with the cooler. When she got back to the car she was annoyed and said, "Why aren't you getting out of the car to puke?" To which I yelled back at her, "I can't get out of the car to puke unless you get me my fucking scooter!" which was the most ridiculous thing I'd ever said in my life. We both started cracking up, and she asked me why I'd eaten so much broccoli.

I didn't puke any more. Thank God, because I really had no idea how I was going to throw up on a scooter in the parking lot of Home Depot. She drove me home and graciously offered to go out without me to get us something to wear for Halloween. I wasn't up to the work it would have taken to finish my costume, which was a toilet.

Yup, that's what I was excited to dress as. I told you I suck at this.

I took a nap when I got home, and three hours later she came back with our costumes. Apparently, it had been a nightmare out there. She had to go all over town and had trouble finding anything appropriate. Also, she likes to be a dick, so I opened the bag with my costume in it to discover that I'd be dressing as Raggedy Andy this year.

"Raggedy Andy?" I asked her. "No wonder you were gone so long. Did you go all the way back to 1975 to get this for me?"

"No," she said. "I went to Goodwill."

Oh, my God (I smelled my costume). I thought it couldn't possibly get worse, until it did. She informed me she'd be going as Captain America. I told you my girlfriend was a dick. I'd be dressing as giant creepy Raggedy Andy in a hideous jumper that smelled funny with yarn for hair, and she'd get to be cute little sexy Captain America? Fuck. Was she still pissed at me for throwing up in her bag?

I rolled on down to the neighborhood Halloween party on my scooter dressed as water park accident Raggedy Andy, complete with the rosy cheeks and freckles my girlfriend felt necessary to add to my face.

It was just another humiliating Halloween. At the end of the night, while my girlfriend was rinsing out her pineapple–clipper ship bag (which she planned to keep on reusing when she got all the broccoli puke out), I asked her if there were other costumes that she could have bought for me. She said, "Just a Dracula one. But I thought that was too easy."

I've had close to fifty Halloweens, and I still haven't been able to pull off a successful cowboy, Dracula, or toilet. But creepy Raggedy Andy with a broken leg? Oh, I knocked that one out of the water park.

it's important to have secure pants

*A*irports are difficult for a person like me: a tall, handsome being with a confident walk and a knack for looking dapper in men's clothes. It gets confusing for folks, so I'm going to give TSA a lot of credit here, because I know they have to look at thousands of people a day and when they call me sir every single time I visit an airport, it's only because I have short hair and am so very muscular. Plus, I'm used to being called sir, so it's really not that big of a deal anymore. In fact, these days I expect it.

I've not always been so comfortable with people calling me sir. It used to make me feel angry, self-conscious, and embarrassed, like they found out a secret that I was trying ineffectively to hide. This was before I grew into myself and realized I have nothing to hide. I began blatantly shopping in the men's department at Nordstrom and stopped feeling weird about walking into the men's dressing room because I was only going in to try on a tie or a shirt. My underpants were staying on the entire time. Plus: doors.

Ten years ago I didn't feel so comfortable. I believe I was even still wearing eyeliner occasionally. That's when I flew to Mexico for a vacation. After five days on the beach in Cozumel I was looking especially masculine, I guess. Perhaps because all of my eyeliner had worn off, and also because of all the beer I'd consumed over the last five days. I also had on a baseball hat. It didn't help that it was on backwards. While waiting for my flight home to the States, I needed to use the bathroom, so I started walking confidently toward the women's restroom, because that is the best option for me. As I got closer to the door, I heard a woman yelling something in Spanish over the regular airport noise, but I didn't see who she was yelling at or even listen to what she was yelling because I was just thinking about going to the bathroom—hey, I didn't stop drinking beer just because I was going home.

The closer I got to that door, the louder the yelling became, and I realized someone was also running toward me. A Mexican airport is the last place you want to hear undue commotion, so I turned around to see what was happening. I immediately saw the female security guard rushing toward me, looking at me with one hand on her belt full of jangling keys and the other in the air pointing at the door to the bathroom while yelling, "Mujeres! Mujeres!" Oh. Fuck.

She was coming at me to emergently and loudly inform me that this was the bathroom for women, stupid gringo, and I shouldn't be walking toward it with all of my handsomeness and intent to pee in the wrong place. She was clearly very concerned with keeping the airport safe one sunburned young man at a time.

This both embarrassed and infuriated me. Not just because of her, but because I realized that the airport had suddenly become silent and aware of me. I stuck out my chest, pointed to my unremarkable boobs, and yelled back, "Mujeres!" She abruptly stopped running, and while everyone in the airport stared at both of us, I turned my baseball hat around to the right way and walked defiantly into the bathroom to hide in a stall until my plane was ready to board. I sat for quite a while in there and wished someone would bring me a beer.

■ ■ ■

I used to wear cargo pants when I traveled because I could put a lot of stuff in the pockets for easy access. Like tampons. I don't carry a purse, so the cargo pockets are a great place for me to put my tampons when I need them, which I did before I went to the airport for yet another trip to Mexico.

I was standing in line holding my shoes, waiting to go through the scanner. The TSA officer was shouting at us, "Please empty your pockets! Take your shoes off and remove laptops from your bags." The standard stuff, but suddenly I realized that my pockets were stuffed with tampons, and no way was I going to pull them out in that line and put them in a plastic bin for everyone to see. I've been embarrassed about getting my period for my entire adult life and don't want anyone to know that I need tampons. I remember going to the pharmacy one late night for tampons and also picking up a bottle of wine and some cat food, just so the clerk wouldn't know what was up. He looked at my items and said to me, "Looks like someone is having a party." Really, Travis? Should I end you now or after I stuff this can of Friskies up your ass?

Some of my girlfriends have capitalized on my tampon-buying phobia by walking down the feminine hygiene aisle with me at Walgreens and shouting, "You need the super plus ones, right, Holly?" Assholes, all of them.

The thought of just putting my tampons on display to have their own Holly Has Her Period Parade while they smiled and waved their way down the conveyer belt and through the scanner mortified me. I kept them in my pockets and hoped for the best. This was the absolute wrong move.

I walked through the scanner while my pockets full of tampons went crinkle-crinkle from all the plastic wrappers. I heard the alarm go off when I walked through, and the TSA agent asked if I had anything in my pockets, sir. At which point I stopped the entire security line to pull out about seven tampons from my pockets while everyone watched me and wondered, *Why does this young man have all these tampons?* The TSA agent then inspected and patted down all of my tampons with everyone watching to make sure they were real and not the most ironic terrorist bombs ever.

After that, I stopped wearing cargo pants to airports and started just wearing my regular pants, which are men's jeans, because I have less curves than are required to make women's jeans look anything but silly and also too short on me. Every time I wear them through security at the airport, though, I set the alarm off. When I look at the screen to see where on my body it's alarming, it's always the crotch area. TSA then has to pat me down. They frequently call for a man to pat me down, and then it gets embarrassing again when they realize their mistake and stumble all over themselves to apologize and try to make me and them feel better about it. It's okay, TSA. I'm aware that I look this way.

For the record, I never actually wear The Jaguar when I'm travelling. You can't sit down in pants in that thing, in case you were wondering. Otherwise I might, because you never know whom you might meet on a plane.

The last time I set off the alarm, while the agent was patting me down and had her hand inside the waistband of my pants, I finally asked why my crotch kept getting flagged. She said it was because my pants have a lot of empty space there. In my head I was all, *Fuck you, I am aware of this,* but I felt it would just make things more awkward if I were to actually say this while she had her hand down my pants. Instead, I just said, "Well, you have an interesting job."

"Pull your pants up higher or wear something tighter if you don't want this to happen every time, ma'am," is what she said. So, basically, I should dress like either a grandpa or a hooker while travelling to not get flagged. Or maybe I could just grow my dick already, security lady, so my life could be a little less humiliating at the airport. And that's "sir" to you.

becoming
kate winslet

I have spent my whole life running away from my womanhood. More specifically, I've been running away from my vagina. I've cursed it since I can remember, have prayed to God to take it away from me, have spent tons of money on clothes and other attachments to betray its existence. The thing is, no matter how fast or hard you run, you can't run away from your vagina. Like an annoying little sister, no matter where you go, it goes with you.

This is the story of my vagina and me.

We'll start this tale back in 1983. I'm fourteen years old, an awkward high school freshman with long feathered hair, straight A's, and a clutch purse that I had no idea where to put. It wouldn't fit in my back pocket, so I tried to kind of perch it on top of my books, which all had glossy covers. What I'm saying is my clutch purse spent a lot of time slipping and falling on the ground. Who thought up clutch purses, anyway? Put a fucking handle on shit, for God's sake.

Let's set the scene: I'm in my bathroom at home sitting on the toilet staring at the instructions from a box of tampons. My hands are sweaty and shaking. My butt is getting sore from sitting, because I've been sitting in there for a long time. At this point I know I have a vagina, but I have no actual idea where it is, except that it's somewhere down there. I've certainly never put anything into it before. Here I am with this tampon in my hand, looking at the diagram on the paper, taking lots of deep breaths, trying to "relax the muscles in the vagina for comfortable insertion," as the instructions say while attempting to locate exactly where my really relaxed vagina might be. Maybe it was vacationing in the Caribbean while I sat on a cold toilet seat in Nebraska.

It was like a game of cornhole that I lost over and over. I don't know how long I sat there trying. It might have been all of spring break. But finally, by some stroke of luck or perhaps the skill of my underhand softball-pitching arm, I achieved success—if you describe success as both the physical and the psychological discomfort that resulted from me finding my vagina. I got up off the toilet, massaged life back into my butt cheeks that were red and asleep, and attempted to ignore what I'd just done to myself. I was both proud and sickened that I'd mastered this part of womanhood and could get back to staring at my Charlie's Angels trading cards and oiling my softball glove.

Up to that point, I had never looked at my vagina, and I made it through that day also without doing so. Why the hell would I want to look at my vagina? I've hated the idea of it since I can remember. If I'd been born with a penis like I was supposed to be, I'd have gazed at it adoringly, told it how amazing it was, complimented its hair and jewelry, and asked about its day. But no, I wasn't given what I wanted. What I was given was a stupid vagina. I was mad as hell about it and had absolutely no inclination to get to know it.

And that's pretty much how it went for my vagina and me for a while. I got better at playing cornhole, but I never got better at carrying a clutch purse. My vagina and I were like roommates that live together but dislike each other. I knew it was there, but I didn't want to be its friend or hang out with it. Even when I started having sex, I didn't have any interest in my vagina, aside from it feeling nice when boys, and then girls, put things into it. I still wanted a penis and fantasized about having one all of the time, but if a vagina was what God gave me, I would begrudgingly use it to feel good. And I did. It turns out I have one slutty vagina. I got very skilled at showing people exactly where it was, but I still hadn't looked at it myself. I looked at everyone else's, and I adored them all. In fact, I was obsessed with looking at all my girlfriends' vaginas. They were all beautiful. It turned me on to just stare at them because I'm pretty gay or a pervy straight dude or something. But I never checked out my own. Not ever. I didn't look at my vagina until I was forty-four years old.

What changed, you ask? Well, I met a girl who believes in being direct, in facing everything, in looking at her vagina. So, on a normal night in September, she glared in dismay at the news that I'd never actually seen my own vagina. How could this be? Also, how could she fix this? I will tell you that my girlfriend is very good at managing people. That night she managed to get me to finally look at my vagina. Basically, she said, "You're going to look at your vagina."

She got out of bed and brought the full-length mirror in from the spare room. She turned on the light and laid the mirror on the floor lengthwise and instructed me to take my underwear off and get down on the floor with her. I complied. As I said, she's a very good manager. Then, against my better judgment, I put my knees up and looked at my vagina. And the very first thought that came into my head was, *She looks very familiar.*

I had seen this vagina before. It was uncanny. In fact, I'd seen it a million times over the years in every porno I'd ever watched. Because I learned that night that's what I have: a porn-star vagina. It was beautiful. I won't get into the details, because I don't want to share too much with you, but it was small and perfect and made for either a lifetime of bicycle riding or a lifetime of hot lights and visits from the cable company that end in surprise gang bangs. It was ridiculous. How had I not seen this before? I'd spent so much of my life as a connoisseur of vaginas. I'd seen so many, and I loved so many. And now I find out that I own one this pretty? It's been living right here in my house with me the entire time?

I sat there staring at it, and I'm a little embarrassed to admit that maybe I got a boner from looking at my own vagina. It must have shown on my face, because the girl elbowed me in the arm and said, "I know. It's pretty good, right?"

Yes, it's good. It's embarrassing how good it is. God has a pretty fucked-up sense of humor. To think all I've ever wanted was a nice shiny black penis, and instead he thought it would be fun to give me this. It wasn't fair. I'd gotten so good at dealing with my biological fate. I'd made it to forty-four by learning to live with what I had, by growing a pompadour and muscles and a cock-sure attitude. By buying strap-ons and getting blow jobs. I'd learned to handle everything God threw at me, but I never saw this coming.

I lay there on the floor staring at it, thinking all of these things about God and irony and porn and gang bangs, getting turned on and upset and proud and uncomfortable all at the same time. I lay there and knew my life would be forever changed by what I had seen that night.

At the age of forty-four, I could describe myself as a gender dysphoric girl-boy nicknamed Steve with a gorgeous vagina. But here's the thing: God keeps fucking with me. It's like I'm his ongoing experiment. Shortly after I realized the tremendous beauty that lives within my pants, my girlfriend took me shopping. We tried on all the clothes at Nordstrom, and I, as I often do, came home with a new button-down shirt, a smart little vest, and a bow tie. Maybe I gave the girl a little fashion show when we got home. Maybe I got laid wearing a shirt, a vest, a bow tie, and glasses, because the girl may have a secret thing for Orville Redenbacher.

That afternoon, Mr. Redenbacher popped his girlfriend, then the glasses and the strap-on came off and my girlfriend turned me on my stomach. With my face buried in the pillow she did a great job of managing me again. When we were done, I realized that I was lying in a pool of wetness that covered so much real estate that it could only mean one thing: I had squirted.

That had never happened to me before. Now I was a squirter. Apparently, my pretty little vagina is growing into herself, finding her voice, asserting herself in my life and all over my sheets. My pretty little vagina will not be ignored. She will not be kept behind the fake dick forever. It's her time to shine. Now she likes to be shaved and exfoliated and moisturized. She wants to go to sleep early so she doesn't look puffy in the morning. She's turning into quite the diva.

And as if that wasn't bad enough, my body is changing in ways I hadn't anticipated. As I get older, my adolescent boy hormones and muscles are fading, and my body has decided to start growing breasts to go with my beautiful squirting vagina. Why, God? Seriously, my boobs are starting to look amazing, which horrifies me. It's like I'm a forty-four-year-old dude but my boobs are seventeen, just had a great time at the puberty party, and are excited to try out for cheerleading this year. Walking naked past the bathroom mirror these days is like meeting someone new for the first time, and she's really hot from the neck down. And of course, my girlfriend loves all of this, because she's pretty gay.

I was lying naked in bed not long ago when she remarked, "You look just like Kate Winslet when she was in *Titanic*, lying in bed with that big necklace on." I told you my girlfriend is kind of a dick.

So now, to add insult to injury, I get to be the curvy one. Perhaps standing on the bow of an enormous ship with my shawl and my breasts billowing out around me, my sexy vagina tucked up tightly, the spray coming up around us either from the ocean or from out of my vagina, my tiny girlfriend grasping me from behind as the wind whips through our hair (but mine doesn't move).

I may end up being a hot, wet female, but at least I don't have to fuck Leonardo DiCaprio, and the closest I'll ever have to come to a glacial swim is when I roll over into the enormous wet spot on my bed. Why is it always so cold?

bowling for significance

I've never been a fan of bowling. What is bowling, anyway? A person in slippery shoes rolls a ball down a lane to knock over some pins. It's called a "sport," yet there are no opponents making it more difficult, the pins don't move, and you don't even have to go down there to get your ball back. It simply reappears. That's not a sport, people.

When I was a kid and my parents took us on Saturdays to the local alley, I was not impressed. I was bored. It was too loud. Everyone gorged on fried food and was way too excited about what wasn't happening. When my dad joined a league, bought a ball, and had his name engraved on it, I was horrified. His official status as My Hero became overshadowed by the image of him working on his spin, which he could never get right, even though there are no variables in the game. Not even wind.

As you can see, I don't really care for bowling.

I'm reluctant to admit this, but I went bowling with some friends a while back (it was probably raining), and I was having a marginally good time. Somewhere around the fourth frame I had this moment: I stood there at the top of that lane, cradling my eight-pound pink ball in both hands, staring at those pins, and time stopped. I thought about the whole of my life and all of the things I'd done and all the great people I'd met—how everything conspired to bring me my current circumstances. It was magical and Zen-like and strange, and I imagined that this frame was somehow a metaphor for my whole life. Really, that's what I thought.

When I brought that ball back and sent it down the alley, I fully expected a strike. I expected those pins to careen and shatter as if a blazing pink destiny rocket had hit them. I expected to turn to my applauding friends and tell them about the enormity of what had just happened. What I did not expect was a seven. A *seven*.

abomination vs. the constitution

I was born on June 26, 1969, in Buffalo, New York. The doctor pulled me out into the brightness and handed me to my mother saying, "Looks like you have the next linebacker for the Buffalo Bills here." At nearly ten pounds I was more than a little big-boned, and my dad still likes to tease me about it. When I walk into a room, he likes to say, "Lookie, lookie. Here comes Cookie," for Cookie Gilchrist, who played for the Bills in 1969. He thinks he's funny.

I grew up like any other kid who was either pretty gay or more likely trapped in the wrong body. I hid and played along, thinking at some point I was going to have to live with Laverne and Shirley and marry either Lenny or Squiggy so no one would think anything was wrong with me. What happened instead was I met this guy named Gary when I was twenty. If I had to be with a man, at least I could be with one who had a lifted pickup to accommodate his height and drove me out to the desert to hike and shoot at things. When he took me to Rosarito Beach, Mexico, and got on his knee to ask me to marry him while I was wearing a giant fringey straw hat, I didn't think twice about saying yes. He was so much cuter than either Lenny or Squiggy.

I said yes to Gary because I didn't know any better at the time, and my parents clasped their hands together under their chins and gasped with joy. I would be taken care of. I'd get a Costco membership. I'd learn to use a crockpot. They would have grandchildren and those kids would be fucking tall.

I felt like all of my struggles with who I was would be over if I got married. It was an escape, a remedy, and I tried hard to believe it. All of our friends were young married couples who were succeeding at work and buying houses with incredible sound systems for blasting Metallica—living the apparently perfect life. It was attractive to be a part of that. It was one big lidocaine shot that numbed the part of me that dreamed about kissing girls and secretly blasted the Indigo Girls on our sound system while Gary was at work. Even our cat knew the lyrics to "Galileo." (P.S.: You can't actually blast the Indigo Girls.)

I was numbed into submission and stayed engaged for over a year, until all of a sudden it wasn't enough. This perfect life was not enough. I knew it was over literally in one second. Fuck. I couldn't marry him any more than I could listen to Metallica for another second. Adiós, normal life.

Now I'm deeply steeped in Homoville and engaged to be married once again. No one really cares about gay people anymore, except in the Republican Party, where they lose their minds over the gays on a daily basis. They obviously have nothing better—like poverty or guns or Walmart—to worry about.

I feel great about getting married this time, because it's not about society and trying to fit in and be normal and make my parents happy. I got over my life being about anyone else's happiness the day I walked out of Gary's front door. This time it's for me.

She is my person. She understands my fucked-up sense of humor, because it's the same as hers. She is smarter than me, but she has the penmanship of a fifth grader, because I don't know why. She folds my underwear just the way I like. Yes, I like my underwear folded. Sure, she talks a lot, but she's also hot as fuck. We've been through the deaths of parents, depression, addiction, and unemployment. We fight over some stupid shit, but never once have I thought, *Nah*. We both love Justin Bieber and '90s country music but hate Mumford & Sons. So, of course I want to marry and build the rest of my life with her. When I asked her, she said yes, and now we are preparing by asking each other the hard questions, like how much porn do you actually watch? What kind should we watch tonight? But there's another reason why I want to get married.

You remember The Jaguar? Well, a few months ago my fiancée told me, "Holly, The Jaguar sometimes hurts me." Wait. What?!

Yes, she said. The material it's made of pulls at the inside of her, and the metal ring that holds the dildo in place slams into her sensitive parts and doesn't feel good. Almost two years in and she just now tells me she doesn't like my dick? Why didn't she tell me before?

She didn't tell me because it's The Jaguar. It's nearly a part of me. How could she tell me that she didn't like this thing that's practically a part of me?

I value my relationship with my fiancée a hell of a lot more than I value The Jaguar, because who else am I going to find in Austin that hates Mumford & Sons? I certainly want her to be happy to have sex with me more than I need The Jaguar. We started looking online at some dildos made of VixSkin, which is supposed to be nicer and softer on a woman's insides. Also, we looked at ones that had, um, balls to protect her from the metal ring. We found the perfect one, but guess what? It didn't come in black. It only came in Caucasian or chocolate brown, because the people that make these things understand nothing about me. I chose the brown one, because if it wasn't shiny and sleek and black, at least it looked a little heartier, like maybe it had worked outside a time or two and wouldn't pull a muscle or get a blister the first time I used it. When it arrived, it was a big, softish brown dick with balls. Apparently, I'll do anything for my lady.

We were picking it up and playing around with it one night when I said, "What should we name this thing? What's big and brown?" Of course she came up with the perfect name: "The Station Wagon." So now, in middle age, I no longer drive a black Jaguar. I drive A WOODY.

One night, we had some hot sex scheduled, because yes, hot sex sometimes needs to be scheduled. (While we're on the subject, sometimes mediocre sex needs to be scheduled too, or sometimes rescheduled, or sometimes you miss your appointment completely and accidentally pass out watching HGTV. It's called life.) As I was the first one out of the shower, I did my best to get us ready. I didn't want to be presumptuous about my dick. I wanted it to be available but not in her face. I put it in the master bathroom where I could easily grab it should the time come.

When that time came, she asked, "Where's The Station Wagon?" To which I replied, "It's in the bathroom. On the toilet."

Well, of course it is. The Station Wagon is sitting on the toilet, probably reading the newspaper while The Jaguar is vacationing along the French Riviera in a tiny swimsuit and an expensive pair of sunglasses. The Station Wagon is much more comfortable and has more of a dad bod than the handsome and shiny Jaguar. The Jaguar lives in a plastic Ziploc bag in a nice, Cole Haan shoebox. The Station Wagon, however, lives in a Taco Cabana bag, no shit, because you can't keep VixSkin in plastic. It has to be in paper or else the material gets messed up, and all I had was a Taco Cabana bag, okay? So you know what? When that's what you're driving, it's time to get married.

June 26, 2015 was a Friday. I had the day off from work, so my lady took me out in the morning for coffee and breakfast tacos. We were sitting in the car eating when the first text message hit my phone. It said, "Happy birthday, Holly. Looks like SCOTUS gave you a nice present this year." No way. This wasn't possible. Same-sex marriage became legal on my fucking birthday? The luck!

On my forty-sixth birthday, the country I live in decided that I'm not an abomination. And that even though I'm big-boned and my life doesn't look like the majority of other Americans, I deserve what the Constitution promises to everyone: equal rights. Five beautiful people, led by one eighty-two-year-old badass woman that I would not want angry at me, decided that I don't have to choose between Lenny or Squiggy or even Gary. I can marry my amazing lady—someone who is hot as fuck, who has a loud and incredibly foul mouth, and who also has one sweet vagina where I can park my Station Wagon, legally.

how we built things when we were children

When I was eight, we used to play in my mother's garden. We made roads by dragging our fingers through the dirt, making giant circles around the geraniums and the onions. Our Matchbox cars powered around and over jumps on their way to Nashville or wherever the Dukes of Hazzard lived. *Vroom* noises led to crashes where there were no victims except the occasional unlucky spider. We made houses out of cardboard that Dad had in the garage. The old Pall Mall boxes would wilt down in the wet soil, the Popsicle stick roofs would tip off in the wind, but we didn't care. This is how we built things when we were children. There was no permanent tragedy, nothing that couldn't be refashioned under the geraniums tomorrow.

When I was forty-one, I bought a pocketknife. It came nestled in a plastic clamshell wrapper, and I cut myself using another knife to get it out before I even had a chance to whittle or skin a squirrel. Once I opened the blade, with its shining danger smile glinting in the backyard sunlight, I discovered that these knives can only be closed by pushing a lever with a thumb to bring the blade down—a direct hit upon the other thumb. When I was forty-one, I went to the emergency room for three stitches.

When I was eight, home plate was a worn place in the grass where only the dirt showed through. First base was the pyracantha bush that grew berries in the summer and would catch your shirt with its thorny branches if you did more than brush by it with an open hand. Second base was the birch tree, the one that was missing most of its paper skin around the middle where we'd grab for safety from desperate tags. Third base was a glove or a hat. We all hated third base because it moved. Third base was fickle but could take a good slide. This is how we built things when we were children. In our backyards with what we had, with rules that were understood.

When I was forty-two, I wanted to play horseshoes in my back-yard, so I spent $115 on supplies, spilled fifty pounds of sand in the back of my Hyundai, and hit my thumb while driving one of the stakes into the perfectly measured and squared pits. During my first match, when things were really heating up to a score of nine to nothing, not in my favor, one of my red horseshoes hit the wooden frame that I'd screwed together at a perfect 90-degree angle and cracked exactly in half.

When I was eight, we colored with crayons. Dad brought us reams of heavy white paper from his job, and we sat at the kitchen table while designing our masterpieces. We drew landscapes or cars or hot air balloons, all filled with happy people and sunshine and butterflies. Even the car pictures had butterflies, because this is how we built things when we were children, out of purple and burnt sienna and gold and silver. Out of sunshine and forever smiles.

When I was forty-three, I learned how to cry in the shower. I learned to sit down and let the water beat hot upon my head and mix with the snot and other things coming out of me to travel down the drain to Nashville or wherever the Dukes of Hazzard lived. I learned to get loud and sloppy, secure in the knowledge that only the cat could hear me; his already low opinion of me mattered little. I learned that honoring sadness is a gift. The Universe has linked sadness to joy, and to cut off one is to deprive yourself of the other. That Universe is a fucker and also invented hangovers, if that's any clue as to how maddeningly clever It is.

When I was forty-three, I sat down in my shower and cried until my fingers puckered and my skin was steamy red-hot. I then got out, dried off, stuck my tongue out at my cat, and went about the rest of my day. That afternoon my neighbor decided to wash her car with her kids and invited me over to hang out and drink pink wine with her. For the record, I don't think pink wine is ever the right thing to do, unless you're my dad, who drinks it over ice and doesn't give a shit. But I walked down there anyway.

There they were, kind of washing the car. We'll call it more of an approximation. Mostly they were spraying water at things not anywhere near the car, like some bugs and that one tree over there. Then my neighbor took the hose and sprayed the kids, who squealed and giggled and ran away and came back for more. Water ran into little two-year-old Zoe Plum's green happy-faced galoshes, so that when she bounced around they made this beautiful wet *squoik* sound. And there it was: joy. Beautiful, unfettered joy that arrived unannounced and cupped us all in its capable hands and held us there for just the shiniest minute.

When I was forty-three, I learned that while the Universe is a fucker, It is a fair fucker.

daydream
mercedes
hand job

When I was a kid I wanted to be a lot of things. I wanted to be Fonzie, I wanted to be a cowboy, and for a long time I wanted to be Stefanie Powers' boyfriend. Basically, if there was a cool or nicely dressed man with a pretty girl or a horse nearby, I wanted to be him. If there was a saloon fight or a moderate speed chase in a convertible, even better. Anything was preferable to wearing my stupid Holly Hobbie pajamas and going to bed with my sister when it was still light outside. I would lie awake in my bed and look out the window, devising elaborate stories in my head where I was always heroic and incredibly handsome.

There was, however, one thing that I wanted to be even more than all of these others, even more than I wanted to be a boy. I knew in every tooth, every hair follicle, every cell of my body that this thing was my destiny. It's like I came into this world with it already done, I just had to figure out what it meant.

When my friends were asked what they wanted to be when they grew up, they said astronaut, teacher, or fireman. When I was asked that question, I responded the same way every time.

"I want to be a superstar."

Every single time, that's what I said. I didn't really know what it meant. My mother listened to Carole King and my father listened to Elvis. I pictured my superstardom as some victorious amalgam of them both. I could gyrate on stage in my gold suit and great hair while my fans wept, from the magic of my mere presence as much as from the poignancy of my lyrics. Cheering and crying were always a part of the picture.

I knew I had problems. I knew from a very young age that I was different, and not in a good way. How was I going to be Elvis if I was a girl? If I was a monster? If I was terribly shy? If I was good at reading and penmanship and English class and bad at singing and hair? I was in the wrong body and had all the wrong skills needed to manifest my destiny. This was so unfair.

So I let that feeling of knowing my destiny slip away. It was too big, too unclear, and too frustrating. Having people around me roll their eyes, pat my head, and shine me on when I told them that I was going to be HUGE got to be a real drag. Thanks, dream-crushers. My ideas changed. I got busy playing kickball and memorizing the presidents. I made myself grow up and out of my knowing this thing. My dream of superstardom drifted away like firecracker smoke. I could still smell it for a while, but then it became altogether intangible. It was too hard, and I had other, more pressing, issues to deal with.

I began to think I'd like to have a career in marine biology. All children, at least all that I knew, went through this phase, and I can't figure out why. Maybe it's because we get such a pleasant reaction from our parents when we tell them. We decide when we're twelve that we like dolphins, so we announce, "I'm going to be a marine biologist." Our parents, envisioning a healthy, tanned child with a PhD and a lifetime pass to SeaWorld, widen their eyes in joy, send a thank-you prayer up to the heavens, and gasp, "That's wonderful!" They then tell all their friends at the restaurant where your mom works that you're going to be a scientist, and you think, *No, I'm going to play with dolphins.*

After that, I wanted to be an artist, then a graphic designer, then an archeologist. By that time I was already in college and had to make a decision because my parents were freaking out. So, of course, I went to nursing school, because I have no idea why.

It kind of worked out. It afforded me the opportunity to live anywhere I wanted to live and have four days off a week. Who gets that? I was lulled, for a while, by that, and by numerous dramas with women and houses and a cat that screamed any time I tried to sleep. I kept journals and took writing classes. Though the ideas of superstardom had withered, I did feel like I was put here to say something important. I just had no clue what it was.

I was funny. I had to be funny. I'd learned early on that it was easier to make people laugh than to let anyone think for a second that I was different. If someone laughed at what I said or did, they tended to like me. They wanted to be around me even though I looked completely awkward in my kitten heels and unruly clutch purse. No one cared while they were laughing, so I got really funny.

People began suggesting that I try stand-up comedy. I'd never considered it. I wasn't even a fan of comedy except in books, but what did I know? I took a comedy class and wrote some jokes about how I humped my life-sized Barbie when I was a kid. The last night of the class we had to perform at a comedy club in front of an audience. *Oh, shit.* Why not just ask me to take my clothes off in public? Somehow I did it. I put on my flashiest outfit and stepped on stage, terrified and white-knuckling the microphone. Despite the jokes about Barbie, it went surprisingly well. The first great laugh I got that night miraculously opened up that box where I'd locked up my childhood knowing. I was on a stage in front of a crowd. People were cheering. My hair looked pretty good. It was happening!

I woke up the next day and felt amazing, until I remembered

that I'd taken my pants off at a bar after the show. Then I felt amazing and peaceful again: ill-advised public nudity was nothing compared to taking one small step toward my childhood dream. The realization that I might actually get the chance to live up to my potential wiped away the years of subverted angst I had lived with while giving suppositories, renovating houses, and otherwise trying to ignore my destiny. It sounds silly, but I went to a bookstore that day and bought a coffee cup that said, "Good things happen when you go for it." For years I drank out of that cup and remembered that first night. The memory of that first big laugh propelled me on through tedious open mics, bouts of nervous diarrhea, and late nights full of fried zucchini and cheap beer. Doing comedy is not nearly as glamorous as it sounds.

But it was a great outlet for me. It gave me a purpose for sitting down and writing. All the journals I'd kept over the years became suddenly useful. I combed through all of them looking for ideas for jokes. There were plenty there.

I became a pretty good comedian and was lucky enough to land some nice gigs. I was just fucked up enough, just wry enough, just dependable enough. I said yes to everything, and because of that I got to be up on many stages and make a lot of people laugh. That felt amazing. I amassed an impressive wardrobe of shiny shirts and belt buckles, and I grew my hair to epic proportions. If I worked hard enough, maybe I could become a famous comedian. That seemed like what I'd been waiting for.

Around the time my comedy career started to really take off, I met a girl and got into a serious relationship. And while I dug her, I let it get more serious than it should have because I thought that's what I was supposed to be doing at that point in my life. I was forty, for God's sake, and ready to be settled down. Literally, before I met her, I thought, *It's time to tie up this last end. It's time for me to be in a serious relationship.*

Then very little about my life was based on anything real. I was doing comedy for the accolades and the idea of being famous. I was involved with this girl to tick off the last box. Look at me being funny and lovable! I am great! Everyone should be my friend! I was achieving what I thought I wanted to, and I never missed an opportunity to pat myself on the back for it. In my head I was earning a first-place trophy for most awesome life in the world.

I went on fooling myself for a while. My popularity grew, I was getting paid to tell jokes, and my girlfriend and I bought white dishes at Crate and Barrel. Everyone knows white dishes are the serious ones. The thing is, despite all of this, I couldn't fool the Universe, which I've pointed out is a Fucker. It had a terrific way of smacking me down.

After two years of playing at this relationship and using this nice woman to help me fit my life into my ideal—while not being really happy with it or participating the way a person should, beyond buying the dishes *and* a salad spinner—I left the relationship and blamed it all on her. Or rather, I kicked her out of the house and began playing new music and blissfully humming in the halls while she packed her things. That's what folks who think they're on their way to becoming Elvis do. None of this could be my fault, right? I'm still great! New girls are buying me beers! I'm cracking them up!

Shortly after I broke up with that girlfriend, I began dating again. Because I still wasn't looking at the reasons why things with my ex went down the way they had, everything was fantastic. I painted my bedroom lavender. I got new crisp white sheets. I bought a leather jacket. I was really moving forward, people. Even if my relationship had failed, I could easily move on to bigger and better things with women. I could still keep my trophy for comedy.

I made it into the Boston Comedy Festival, which was the most important thing I'd been invited to do up to that point. Boston was the big time, and I made sure to brag to everyone I knew about it.

Since I was the Big Shit, I decided to take a new girlfriend with me to show her just how amazing I was; I was sure my Comedy Central special couldn't be far behind.

The night of the festival, I expected to kill while dressed in my nicest vest and smart bow tie, à la the scholarly Northeast. Instead, I ate shit on stage.

It was worse than the time I got booed in Portland for telling a Mexican joke (do not tell any race jokes in Portland. They will murder you, cut you up into little pieces, and recycle you into bicycle parts). I ate it hard right there in front of new girl and the city of Boston. I'd built myself up to such epic proportions and thought I would easily slay, but then this thing happened instead. I gathered the sweaty, deflated pieces of myself together and moped angrily out into the rain back to the studio Airbnb we'd rented.

We still had six days left in Boston, which would have been great if she hadn't ignore-dumped me immediately after I bombed. Ignore-dump is when someone has clearly made up her mind to not be with you, since you aren't the superstar you've made yourself out to be, but she doesn't tell you. You can feel it, and you keep asking her why she won't touch or really even look at you, but she says everything is okay because she wants to stay in Boston and you already paid for the room and her airfare. It's like ghosting, but face-to-face and more awkward. Even though we shared a queen-sized bed, I wasn't allowed to get too close to her, and in the mornings I had to go out by myself in the rain to give her some alone time to get ready to ignore me some more. Best ignore-dump ever.

When we got home, she for real dumped me over a game of Bananagrams. This is when my mojo packed up all its shit and left me. Adiós, Holly's mojo. I started feeling sorry for myself. I was angry and bitter at my turn of circumstances. All the girls ditched me. I found myself alone much of the time because suddenly no one wanted to be around me. I started bombing. And bombing. And bombing. I was stringing the bad sets together like rotting fence pickets, one after another. It got so bad that the owner of the comedy club where I was a regular called me to ask what was wrong, because it didn't look to her like I had any confidence. Comedy club owners don't generally call you—they just stop booking you and move along to the next dependable person—but that's how worried about me she was. Whatever gift I had was seemingly gone. How did this happen? I'd been killing on stage for five years and now suddenly I sucked? What about my destiny?

My self-esteem tanked. I started drinking way too much. I chipped a tooth one night and decided it was a good idea to file it down with a nail file. I woke up one morning with broken glass in my hair and my back and absolutely no recollection of how it got there. I was lonely, defeated, and slowly realizing that what I thought would get me the one thing I wanted most in life wasn't going to work.

Why not? Because, like my failed relationship, it was a sham. It wasn't real. I had been on stage doing everything I could to get people to think I was great, to not actually see me, and it was finally falling apart. Fucking Universe.

On a cold afternoon in February, after this had gone on for months, feeling empty of everything but sadness, I sat down in my shower and turned the water on hot, cradling my forehead in my hands under the water, crying about what was happening to me. I thought about the fact that my friends didn't want to be around me the way I was. Audiences didn't want to laugh at me anymore. The act I was putting on, in life and on stage, wasn't working anymore. I was trying, with the jokes and the outfits and the hair, to win over the world, to get everyone to like me, and it was all crashing down around me because it wasn't real. It either had to end, or I was going to spend the rest of my life crying in this ugly shower with the peeling paint and shitty water pressure. When I couldn't cry anymore, when I was all wiped out and peaceful, I made a decision:

I was going to drop the act and just be real. I was going to stop my whole song and dance and just be myself. If people didn't like it, at least it would be real.

I decided that I wasn't going to do stand-up any more. I finally admitted it to myself that telling jokes wasn't being honest or doing what I was put here to do. I was tired of selling out the sensitive parts of myself for cheap punch lines. I gave myself a different assignment: write the most difficult and personal story I could, and find a way to tell that to people. When I thought about the possibilities, I quickly knew that it could only be about one thing, something I'd been previously too embarrassed to talk much about. I would write about my gender problem and feeling like a monster for most of my life.

A friend of mine produces a show called *BedPost Confessions*, where people get up and tell their stories about sex, gender, and sexuality. Right when I got out of the shower, I sent her an e-mail asking, if I wrote this, would she let me tell it there? I was terrified at the prospect of revealing something so personal in front of strangers. I'd been ashamed of this stuff for most of my life. But if I was going to do this, I was going to do it all the way. She kindly agreed to put me on the show. Suddenly, I had a deadline.

I sat down to write, and the story poured out of me. I remembered things I'd stuffed away long ago. I sat and typed at my computer with a box of Kleenex next to me for all the crying I was doing. I felt like someone was digging giant chunks of buried shame out of me and laying them all around for me to look at. How had I not thought about all of this for so long? It shaped the entirety of my life.

When it was done, I finally understood why I'd put so much effort into creating my false existence. This shit was scarier than I remembered. I'd begun hiding who I was at an early age, and it eventually carried over into every aspect of my adult life. I spent two months writing and crying and finally falling in love with the little monster that I had felt like as a child. I also began to like the adult I had grown into. That felt so nice, and so new to me. Still, I fretted about the approach of the show. What would happen? I'd be up on a stage, completely vulnerable, telling secrets that I'd buried a whole lifetime ago. There were no punch lines. There would be no more hiding.

The day of the show, April 12, 2012, I was so nervous I made myself sick. I'd spent years getting up in front of people on a stage and I'd gotten used to the stress of it, but now I was so mortified I couldn't get out of the bathroom the whole day. This was going to be so much worse than taking my clothes off in public, but I knew I had to do it.

That night I got up on stage and read my story. I was so scared that I paid absolutely no attention to the audience's reaction. When I was through, I quickly turned to walk off the stage but was stopped short by my friend, the producer. She told me, "Go back. They're giving you a standing ovation."

I turned around and there they were: two hundred people standing up and cheering for me. I'd been at home all day puking and having diarrhea about what I was going to do that night, and then this. They were cheering and crying! The cheering and crying of my childhood dreams! The tears poured out of me. It was the most amazing thing I've ever felt—cathartic and moving. I'd shown these strangers all the scary and shameful parts of me, and they loved me for it. That night was the catalyst for a lot of these stories. It was also the catalyst for me getting back up on stages. Not to tell jokes, but to tell real stories. Now when I'm lucky enough to again get cheering and crying, I know that I'm finally aimed straight arrow at my destiny. That feels incredible.

I've since gone back and watched video of my comedy sets. What I see when I watch is someone who is throwing a voice, jumping and waving hands around, doing everything possible to distract everyone from seeing who is actually standing on that stage: a quiet, shy, sensitive girl/boy full of insecurity and in desperate need of love. It makes me sad. I want to scream into the screen, "Just stop it and be yourself!" But I guess there had to be some mysterious shards of glass and crying first.

During my mojo-free winter, about the only friend who would spend time with me was my buddy Kathrin (God bless you, Kathrin). One afternoon we were sitting around drinking beer and talking about our lives. She told me a story about how she grew up in an affluent neighborhood in Connecticut where she felt like an outsider. She was dealing with the same kind of shame that I was, dreaming the same dreams of having a big life. She would walk the streets of her neighborhood, lonely, hoping a shiny Mercedes would pull up next to her, roll down the window, and offer her all the fame and fortune she dreamed of.

What we both thought we wanted was fame. We thought fame would be the magic bullet to make people like us. But what we realized when we were talking that day is that what we actually wanted was to be free of our shame. We wanted someone to tell us that we were okay the way we were. I said to her, "Kathrin, no one is going to pull up alongside of us in a nice car and roll down the window to offer that to us. The only thing anyone in that car would likely offer us is money for a hand job."

I don't want hand job money, and not just because it would be a shitty, Indian sunburn, discount hand job. It's that I don't need fame or superstardom anymore. What I want is to be a person who stands in my truth and is loved, or not, for exactly that. I want this for all of us. We are all little monsters struggling with our shame and self-loathing. If we'd all tell the truth and show our real selves, we'd realize that we are all basically the same, and none of us are alone in our struggling. We could all stop pretending and finally show up to cheer and cry for each other together. And anyone who wanted a hand job could probably get one for free!

Tammy's shirt was up, pushed up as high under her arms as it would go. It was August and her skin smelled like the sun that was shining outside. The shades in the trailer were drawn against the afternoon glare and I had her there in the dark, up against the door. There was a mirror on the outside of it, and in its reflection I saw myself nervously exploring what was under her shirt with my hands and mouth. I was nervous not only because I knew that what I was doing was wrong, but also because I feared our parents would come back from the lake to check on us to make sure I didn't have my best friend, Tammy, pressed up against the closet door with her shirt up and my mouth all over her virgin parts. We were four years old.

It started as an idea Tammy had. "Let's play boyfriend and girlfriend," she suggested. I didn't even know that was a game, but you bet I was going to play. I was most definitely going to be the boyfriend.

Ever since I can remember anything about my life, I've known I was supposed to be a boy. It wasn't a decision I made in my head; there was no logic, no reason to it. It just was. I identified with the boys on TV, and I was particularly obsessed with Fonzie. I wanted his awesome life, and I fantasized about having a motor-cycle, muscles, and a fist that could jump-start a jukebox. I'd sneak into the bathroom and with a wet comb try to coax my hair into a blonde pompadour while giving the thumbs-up and saying "Hhhhheeeeeeyyyyy."

I only wanted to play with my brother's toys, Matchbox cars and GI Joe dolls. I wanted to wear boy clothes, in particular white T-shirts with the sleeves rolled up and cowboy hats. When my brother and sister and I played house, I always wanted to be the dad, which was fine with my brother, who always wanted to be the dog. I couldn't ever imagine being a girl, especially during make-believe when I got to choose what I was.

When Tammy offered to let me be her pretend boyfriend, you bet your ass I did it. How did I know, at four years of age, what boyfriends did to girlfriends? Well, I certainly had a good idea about what to perpetrate up there under her shirt, and it was the best make-believe EVER. I don't remember it being sexually erotic. My plumbing couldn't have been all hooked up yet. But enjoy it I did. Because for however long we were hidden away in that dark trailer, I got to be a boy. With a girl. And even though I was only four, I was digging the hell out of it. Fonzie had nothing on me that afternoon.

As I got older, I realized that I had a serious problem: make-be-lieve was not real life. It dawned on me that who I was on the outside and who I was on the inside didn't match. I didn't just *want* to be a boy. I knew I *was* a boy, except where everyone could see. All the rolled up white T-shirts and cowboy hats wouldn't change it. I was named Holly, I had to wear curlers in my hair every year the night before class pictures, and I had to take gymnastics in PE with the girls instead of baseball with the boys.

What happened? What was wrong with me? Everyone else seemed to be just fine with who they were. My brother certainly matched. You could tell because he was gross and didn't mind drinking out of a water bowl on the floor when we played house. My sister was happy to have long hair and wear pretty clothes and curlers and be the mom. I was jealous and confused and keenly aware that I wasn't right, not just because I was the only girl in class who couldn't do a goddamned cartwheel. All of it was just humiliating.

My mom was Catholic, and she taught us that God made things how they are and that we could have anything we wanted if we just prayed about it. This was God's fault, then. I knew all those scary prayers they taught us about dying before I woke up and having my soul taken, and I used to lie in my bed saying them over and over to prove to God how good I was. Then I'd plead with him to work his God magic overnight and let me wake up as a boy. I'd pray so hard, with my eyes scrunched closed and my hands forced together with an urgency that could not possibly be ignored. *Please, God, please.* In the mornings I'd wake up and lie absolutely still to see if I felt differently. I'd wait as long as I could before I opened my eyes to check.

The disappointment was new and crushing every single time. God hated me. He did this to me. Before I was born, he switched me into the wrong body and was certainly punishing me for something by not changing me back. I was obviously the only one in the world this had happened to, and the shame of that was overwhelming. I knew and God knew that I was a monster. But no one else was ever going to know, I vowed, because no one could love a monster.

Time went by, and I used my secret boy-ness to win at softball and basketball and fights with boys on the playground. I started being immensely interested in girls—their bodies, their hair, and the way they smelled. Some of my friends were growing into their pretty selves, and it made me feel funny and nervous to be around them. I watched *Hart to Hart* on TV and thought Stefanie Powers was the most magnificent girl I'd ever seen. She played Jennifer Hart, who was a freelance journalist who never wrote anything because she was too busy flying on jets with her husband, played by Robert Wagner, to solve cases of espionage and murder. When criminals tried to give her shit, she shot them with a tiny stylish pistol that she kept in her purse. When she kissed Robert Wagner, a bomb went off in my pants that sent tingling shrapnel throughout my body. I didn't understand what was happening. I mean, I was supposed to be watching handsome Robert Wagner when they kissed, right? And fantasizing that I was Stefanie Powers, like a normal girl. But instead, I couldn't stop staring at Stefanie Powers and feeling funny. I officially started fantasizing about being Robert Wagner, wearing a white tuxedo jacket, driving home in my green convertible Mercedes after solving just slightly interesting criminal cases with my beautiful wife, who would of course let me kiss her in our castle.

When my mom told us about how babies were made, she said that a man plants his seed in the woman he loves and then that makes a baby. Sex sounded an awful lot like farming. I imagined rows and rows of tiny babies sprouting from the earth while chickens scratched around and Charlotte spun webs in the barn. But how I really learned about sex was when I had my first sex dream. In it I was a boy with a penis. I put it into a girl and sex happened. It was glorious and so much better than farming could ever be. Now I understood what all those funny feelings were about, and I wanted more than ever to not just be a boy but also to have a penis, so I could do that with it in real life. This made me even madder at God for messing up my body. It was bad enough that I couldn't ever grow sideburns, but I never saw the whole penis thing coming. The only good news was that I was incredibly creative and became very skilled at imagining that I actually had one. I started thinking about having sex like that all the time. Poor Stefanie Powers. I bet she didn't get any sleep in 1980 because in my dreams I was busy all night long sticking it into her.

I knew puberty was coming, and I couldn't bear the thought of it. Growing breasts and getting my period was the antithesis of anything I wanted for myself. I remember sitting around on a Saturday afternoon when my sister ran into the house and up the stairs, calling for my mom. A half hour later, my mom marched dramatically down the stairs, demanded everyone's attention, and announced, "Your sister's a woman now."

I looked up from the game of Connect 4 my brother and I were playing and thought, *What? She was only up there for a half hour.* I had just seen her, but now a half hour later she's suddenly a woman? Is this how it happened? I was doomed. I imagined the arrival of womanhood would be like a house fire, swift and unforgiving, leaving my childhood dreams of muscles and pompadours in carbon ashes scattered in the upstairs bathroom.

I battled puberty with all my might, all my dreams, and all my prayers. But puberty, as it always does, won. It knocked me, defeated, into the upstairs bathroom on a sunny afternoon after I got my period in front of the entire freshman softball team. If I wondered if God hated me before, now I was absolutely certain of that fact. My father, who was the only one home that day, did his best to console me. Poor Dad. He had no idea the extent of the issue. I wasn't just crying because I was embarrassed or because I had cramps. I was crying because it was done. I was officially a woman. God was never going to change me back, and there would be absolutely no more praying about it.

I tried to accept my fate. I tried to pass. I crept through high school, faked liking boys, and tried to carry a purse, all the while knowing that it was a ruse. At night I had dreams that I was a boy having sex with girls. During the day I'd wait for everyone to leave the house so I could turn on the Playboy Channel and hope it would unscramble long enough to make out a blow job scene. The hole where I was stuffing my secrets was getting deeper and deeper. I still hadn't told anyone. How could I? While what was happening inside of me made for some exciting nights in my bed, it certainly wasn't okay with me. It was wrong—bad—and I hated it. I hated myself for it.

I wondered how I would be able to live like this. Even if the issue was that I just liked girls, it was still unacceptable. The only thing I knew about being gay was that it was going to be hard, I was going to hell, and I was going to have to be a softball coach. But my issue was obviously much bigger than just liking girls. I was also stuck in the wrong body, and I had zero cultural references for that. The only exposure I had to anything approximating a display of gender dysphoria was a Duran Duran video. I stayed silent and did my best to keep my invisible penis at bay during many uncomfortable slumber parties with my pretty friends.

I made it to college with my secret and became so good at passing that I suffered a brief brush with prettiness, thanks to an epic perm and my sister's wardrobe. I met a man whom I liked very much, who wanted to marry me, and I thought that maybe things would get better. If I couldn't have a penis, at least I could have

decent sex. Sure, he looked nothing like Stefanie Powers, but I was so horny by this time that it didn't matter. Maybe the dreams and fantasies that battled with my reality would disappear and leave me alone to be normal like everyone else. I was desperate to believe it could.

I got a job waiting tables at a Mexican restaurant. The uniform they gave me to wear was a dress, a billowy off-the-shoulder señora dress with puffy sleeves. I also had to tie my legendary hair back with an enormous yellow bow. I put it all on and went to work. Despite the outfit and all the years of trying to deny and suppress and kill off what was inside of me—despite the prettiness—there was still enough boy in me to make me seem like one giant Mexican cross-dresser. I lumbered up to the tables with my hair and my dress fluttering out behind me and said, "Hola!" I scared the shit out of the customers. It was too much for them, and it was way too much for me. The two days I spent working at that job, coupled with the sensational sex dreams I was currently having about a girl in one of my college classes, rubbed all the warring pieces of me together hard enough to make a crack just big enough to show how silly I looked, how silly I felt.

Right there, amidst the smell of fried corn chips and the sound of accordion music, I decided that denying everything about who I was on the inside just wasn't worth it anymore. I'd had enough. At that point I only had the courage to decide to be with women; I couldn't yet face anything about my gender. I hoped that just being gay would be enough.

I got my amazing perm cut off, broke off my engagement, and had sex with a girl. It was the first time since that afternoon in the trailer with Tammy that I had another girl's shirt up, and this time all of my plumbing was working. Touching and kissing parts of her that were definitely not four years old was almost overwhelming. That night in her bed was the hottest thing I'd ever experienced in my reality, but it was still no

So Hella Gay

Photo by: Suzy Webber

149

comparison to my sex dreams where I was a boy, sometimes sticking it in, but mostly getting blown by all number of beautiful women.

While I gave myself permission to by gay, I still had a big secret that I intended to keep. I went on for years hiding the boy that lived inside of me.

It's not like there wasn't plenty of talk about people struggling with this same issue. I'd seen Jerry Springer a few times and I knew I was no longer alone in how I felt, but I was so used to feeling like a monster, wrong and ugly and ashamed. I didn't want sex and relationships with girls to go away because I told the truth. I kept silent. I was still going to be a girl, dammit. Even in bed.

That all changed the night a girl gave me my first blow job. It started as an idea she had. "Let's play blow job," she said. Well, not exactly, but she had this fantasy of blowing a girl, so she took me to the adult store and let me pick out any penis I wanted. Of course, I chose the black one.

Once I figured out how to put it on, with its intricate menagerie of straps and buckles, I felt an immediate shift in my insides. I had a penis, and it certainly wasn't make-believe now. When this sweet, dirty girl put it into her mouth, my life changed forever. She was there on her knees in front of me with her red hair and brown eyes tilted up at me. With the smell of the vanilla candles and her Calvin Klein perfume all around us, she gave me the longest, slowest, most tender interracial blow job I could ever have imagined. For those twenty minutes, everything except the *kaboom kaboom* of my heartbeat in my ears went away. And though I couldn't feel it physically, I could feel it electric in every other way possible. I had suddenly gotten the one thing in life that I wanted but had given up total hope on. I finally got to feel at home in my physical body. It was the most amazing sexual and nonsexual thing I'd ever experienced. Life could finally match my dreams.

That night, without knowing what I was doing and without it being my idea, I consented to accept the boy who lived inside of me.

It was as if I had a precious twin who had been unfairly banished from my kingdom at birth, who had been wandering alone and tired and scared for thirty years, who was now suddenly allowed back where he belonged. That girl blew my lights out and turned all the lights on inside of me at the same time.

That was the beginning of me admitting to others and becoming comfortable with who I am. My evolution has been a slow process, beginning with just the sex part of it, with strap-on sex toys and girls who liked to play with them. Over the course of years, I began letting it also spill over into the rest of my life. Like fashion. I started shopping for clothes in the men's department at Target and Nordstrom, because *fuck you, señora dress.* This part of it took a lot of my courage. For a while I felt like everyone was staring at me and judging me as I picked through the masculine button-downs, jeans, and even men's underwear (boxer briefs!). I had no problem buying a big black dick for myself at the sex store, but shopping for men's clothes was making me nervous? Silly.

I went to the gym and tried to grow some muscles. I got called sir a lot in public restrooms (thanks for noticing, ladies). I started getting my hair cut at a barbershop. Oh, my God, this one was big. Every time I go, I sit in the chair and giggle excitedly at what I'm doing. When I talk to the barber about it, he or she is always so proud of me. Though I don't have sideburns, I do have a sharp part and a fade that'd make David Beckham jealous.

One recent summer Gillette sent me a razor for my birthday as an advertisement. On the box it said, "Happy eighteenth birthday, Holly. Welcome to manhood." *Squeal!*

While I appreciate the gesture, Gillette, I can't claim that as my entire truth. Here's the thing: while I'm not exactly a female, I'm not exactly a male either. I'm more of a hybrid, I guess. Now that I've had time to live in this body, I don't feel like it's so black and white, and I'm not as mad about it as I was when I was young. I've somehow figured out how to celebrate both sides. Except I never celebrate my period, because that's just dumb and I'm still kind of pissy at God about it. I wear men's jeans because they fit better; I wear women's sports bras because they fit better. Sometimes I wear my big black penis in bed; sometimes I leave it under the bed and take it like a girl. And I still, constantly, have hot dreams about blow jobs.

I hate having to check the gender box on forms. First, why is gender so important? And second, why can't they have more than two boxes? Like ones that say *Other*, or *Undecided*, or *That's a long story*, or *What does it matter*, or *None of your business, asshole,* or maybe *Seahorse*? (Look up the sex lives of seahorses. That shit is interesting.) The thing is, I don't give a fuck anymore. I'm amazing.

A friend told me a story. She said that when her aunt died, her family gathered around her and told her to go to heaven to get her crown. As she was dying, she started patting her head and smiling. I hope when I'm about to die, my family gathers around me and tells me to go to heaven to get my penis. I'll pat my crotch and smile, knowing that God will have one for me, and it'll be big and black, because maybe he doesn't hate me after all.

the man,
the myth,
the legend

I went to nursing school on a whim. I never once in my life thought I wanted to be a nurse, but I had a freak-out moment in college where I needed to make a decision and the nursing building was pretty close to the lot where my parking permit was valid. I told myself when I graduated that I'd give myself five years before doing something else. I've since learned that no other job comes with four days off a week and the ability to wear pajamas to work. As a result, I've stayed in it for twenty-plus years.

If you read these stories in order, you know that I also moved to Texas on a whim. I found my way to a job at a very small hospital because my staffing company said they needed help one Sunday and I wasn't doing anything else. When I pulled into the parking lot, a deer galloped across the cobblestones in front of me. When I got out of my car, I heard dance music lilting out of speakers hung in the beautiful oak trees on the campus. What the fuck kind of hospital was this, with its wildlife and good taste in music? It turns out it's a cool-as-shit one full of beautiful weirdos. That's right, I fit right in. So I stayed.

This hospital is full of patients, sure. But it's also full of fun and dancing. We keep one of those counter bells by the charge nurse, and if you make a particularly sick burn, you get to slap the bell and then someone down the hall will yell, "Order up!" There is constant giggling, especially on Fridays when we hold afternoon dance parties in the social work office and get down to Justin Timberlake or Prince. We would all be fired immediately in a normal hospital, but here we are celebrated, especially if one of us trips while holding a tray of food or walks in on someone who forgot to lock the bathroom door. That's a pretty big celebration.

We also do a great job of taking care of patients, probably because we're all so damned happy most of the time. My specialty was recovering people in the ICU after open-heart surgery. My favorite part about it was that most people did well. They came in, had their surgery, ate pain pills and green Jell-O, got out of bed, walked, laughed at my stupid jokes or when they heard someone yell, "Order up!" and went home with a pillow shaped like a heart. I made my patients all come back on their one-year anniversaries to show me their scars and update me on how they were. My favorite thing to say was, "I almost didn't recognize you with pants on." Clearly, I had found my niche.

After I worked there for five years, the hospital had to eliminate the heart program because it was too small and they couldn't afford to keep it going any longer. I had to decide between going to work for another hospital and staying where I was and never recovering heart patients again. I certainly wasn't going to abandon my counter bell and my Friday Prince dance parties; I love to dance and my jokes need to come out. I decided to stay and figured I could try to find other ways to be happy there, even while just changing knee dressings or walking grandmas with pneumonia to the bathroom twenty-seven times a day, reminding them each time not to grab me with used Kleenex in their hands. Grandmas really like their Kleenex.

Then, something spectacular happened. My boss called me into her office and told me that we were getting a new service line in the coming year that I would probably be excited about. That service line was phalloplasties, which, if you google like I had to, is creating a phallus from a flap of skin taken from another part of the body. Or, if you need it in my type of English, it's the bottom part of female-to-male surgery where *they build a dick that has feeling where there previously was no dick.* So, basically, what I'd wanted for myself for my entire life. Right there in my tiny weirdo hospital in Texas. Where I had no business being. A world-renowned gender reassignment surgeon from San Francisco was putting a team together to operate in Austin, and right in my lap is where they somehow ended up. Like all the whims had planned this the entire time.

I had to google it because I am the worst wannabe-man on the planet and had no idea this was even possible. I'd talked to some of my friends who also wanted dicks about what our options were, and we all thought our only choice would be to take hormones and get what we already had to grow into something that looked more like a thumb than a dick and try to be happy with that. But none of us wanted another thumb. We wanted something that looked real and worked, or else forget it. We were proud girl/boys, all of us, and we didn't want our dicks to be tiny. We had no idea that this whole other thing was happening.

I went home the night I found out, sat on my porch, and told my girlfriend about what was coming. I was stunned and still in disbelief while the birds chirped on like it was just another day in the middle of Texas. My girlfriend looked at me and said, "I can't believe how lucky you are. Everything just works out for you." She obviously hasn't read any of my stories, but I understood what she meant. The serendipity was just a little overwhelming.

The next months flew by in a flurry of Google searches, blog views, and in-service trainings about female-to-male transitions and hormones and using proper pronouns and what it would look like and feel like and how it would feel that way. It wasn't just me doing all of this searching; it was lots of folks at the hospital who probably hadn't even thought much about this stuff before. Now we were all looking at dick pics on a daily basis. The search histories of our work computers must have been a nightmare for the IT and HR departments. I had never been more proud of us.

The day the surgeon flew in to give us his official presentation on what he planned to do, I sat in the audience with my mouth open, mind blown. Here is an explanation of the procedure:

The team takes a flap of tissue from one's nondominant forearm and removes it most of the way. It has blood vessels and some very sensitive forearm nerves in it.

While it is still attached on one end, they roll it up, leaving a hollow channel in the middle that will become the new urethra.

Then, while it's still on the forearm, they make it look real, by doing some magical penis origami shit.

While this is being done, the labia are turned inside out to make little scrotum, and the clitoral nerve is exposed. That's the important part. The arm dick is then carefully transplanted to where a dick should actually be, and the sensitive forearm nerves are connected to the clitoral nerve.

In about nine months, everything heals together, including all those important nerves. This allows for erotic feeling the length of the new dick. I told you this shit was cool. Add a boner implant and *ta da*! Yes, the new dick does everything a dick should do, except ejaculate, which is the gross part anyway.

Here was a medical professional finally recognizing and acknowledging that what I had was a medical diagnosis. Gender dysphoria was an actual thing that was serious enough that people like him had engineered incredibly complicated surgeries to remedy it. Even after spending so much time living with how I was and accepting that this happened, this moment was a big and validating one. I hugged the shit out of that doctor. Then I introduced myself. Not everyone at the hospital knows that I'm in the wrong body. Many just think I'm a silly dyke with a good haircut and a coffee cup that says, "STEVE: The Man, The Myth, The Legend." But my friends there who do know were happy for me and started asking me if I was going to have the surgery.

Was I going to have the surgery? I hadn't even known that it was an option. I just figured I had to tough life out with my cute little vagina. But now here we were making dicks!

As an ICU nurse, it was my job to inspect the new "flaps" (medical term for newly made penis) every hour. I had to listen for pulses and assess color and turgor (firmness) to make sure they were maintaining adequate circulation, which means I had to listen to, squeeze, and *boop* dicks almost constantly. In one month I'd gained exponentially more intimate exposure to dick than in my previous entire life. I had never actually listened to one before.

I got to say things like, "Congratulations! Want to measure it?" (always met with a giant *yes*). And, "Your balls look great!" because I am very professional. I was so pleased that we were doing this for people, and I couldn't help but be excited for them to finally get what they wanted their whole lives. There were many high fives and dick selfies and talks about underwear. I had never met this many people like me before, and I was absolutely reveling in it in between all the dick-booping.

But after the pressure and intensity of the new program settled, I noticed that I was having feelings that were not just happiness and excitement. I noticed that I was feeling jealous. At first, it was just jealousy of how good these guys looked with their top surgeries. All people like me will tell you that while not having a dick is really bad, having boobs is publicly humiliating. Boobs embody everything in our society that is feminine and sexy, and the last thing a dude like me wants is to feel boob-sexy and feminine. One of my greatest desires is to be able to wear a white T-shirt with nothing under it. My boobs keep me from that because they are really nice and perky, and extra humiliating.

I soon started feeling jealous about the whole thing. These guys had the opportunity to overthrow what biology had done to them, and they were brave enough to grab it. They took hormones, changed their names, came out to their families, changed their driver's licenses, grew facial hair, had top surgery, and then underwent an eight-hour surgery to complete themselves and make their outside match their inside. Meanwhile, here I was, busting my ass to take care of them in a room turned up to eighty degrees, and I hadn't even paid myself the respect to consider doing the same for myself, this thing that I'd wanted my whole life. How could I not consider it when it was literally staring me in the face for twelve hours a day?

Which brings us to what I'll now call "The Dark Week," where I became very dramatic and called my friends to each come over and sit on my porch while I cried about how conflicted I was and how terrible it was to be like me. I called my girlfriend who was out of town on business to ask her if she'd still love me if I changed my body, my voice, and potentially became a bald and pimply Steve, as hormones do all kinds of crazy things. I even called the producer of the show I was supposed to be writing a piece for about the sexualization of nurses but couldn't manage to do, because the only thing I could write about nurses was also about dicks and not having one. It really was a dark week, especially for my porch friends.

To answer my question, my girlfriend assured drama queen Steve that yes, even though she would miss my perky amazing boobs, she would love me no matter what, unless I kept being so fucking dramatic. So I stopped being dramatic and just tried to think about what I wanted instead of how cruel God was to me and how terrible my struggle was. This is where I was *now*. Did I want to transition? Did I just want top surgery? Did I want to take hormones or officially change my name to Steve? Did I want the dick that I'd been dreaming about my entire life, except it wouldn't be black like my favorite strap-on and would unfortunately have the word "Dad" written on it thanks to a poorly timed forearm tribute tattoo?

The answer settled on me quietly like snow. The answer was no, I didn't want to change at all. None of it. Maybe if I was twenty or even thirty, the answer might be different. But I'm forty-seven, and that's a long time to have lived with myself. It's not that I'm too old to do it. Some of our patients are over fifty and they have no qualms about charging ahead with the whole thing. And I mean no disrespect to my brothers and sisters who decide to fully transition. It's a deeply personal decision that we all have to make for ourselves. It's just that I've spent my whole life becoming who I am. I've grown up with this struggle, and it has shaped just about every area of my life. Now it's part of my identity to be a tall, gender-dysphoric, handsome girl with a decent sense of style, a better sense of humor, and the nickname Steve. I've grown comfortable here in the middle. Sure, I wish it had been different, that I'd been born in the correct body, that I had a dick that wasn't imaginary, that I could have sex the way I do in my dreams. But then it would be different. Everything would be different. Maybe I'd be just an average-height guy who was going bald and wasn't funny and didn't have any good stories to tell. *Ick*. For me, that's even worse than no dick.

Now I'm back to celebrating surgeries with the patients that have them and feeling proud that I somehow landed in this ironically magical place at the right time to be able to help people with a condition that I understand. We can laugh and share horror stories and marvel at how quickly the world is changing. I have the privilege of being a part of their journey, and that makes me very happy.

I can tell them all to come back and visit me, but that I probably won't recognize them with their pants on. I also get to tell them to text me when they get their first blow job that they can feel, because, as I told you, I am a professional.

I went back to visit my hometown and hung out with some friends I'd known since grade school. We were drinking on a porch, having non-dramatic time, and we all took little Internet tests to determine what animals we are. The Internet told me I am a butterfly. My friends, who had known me for so long and had seen me go through so much, all agreed that I was indeed a butterfly. So now I have a question: Is a caterpillar something that has to change to become a butterfly? Or is a caterpillar always a butterfly that just hasn't grown into it yet? Because caterpillar I certainly was: kind of green and pudgy, ambling around slowly, trying to not get smushed or eaten. But now I'm a goddamned butterfly, and I didn't have to change. I just had to grow into it.

loose change

*T*hirty-seven cents. One quarter, a dime, and two pennies. Loose change. What you might get back if you pay cash for a tallboy at the convenience store, or I don't know, a tube of lipstick. Some coins that you drop into your right front pocket and walk around with. You might hear them jingle occasionally or feel them with your hand when you stick it in there, but mostly they're nothing to you, until you take off your pants at night and go to hang them up and the coins fall all over your closet floor. Then you kick them into the corner because you never pick shit up, and your sweet girlfriend picks them up and puts them somewhere.

Thirty-seven cents represents the hatred I've felt about my body my entire life. Just this thing I carried around in my pocket and would think about only occasionally. Like, if I needed to put on a bathing suit, or had to get a mammogram, or if I tried to buy the shirts I actually wanted at Nordstrom. That's when it would flare up the worst, but even then I just kicked it to the corner of my closet. This is what my body is. I can deal with it.

I've told you about my dick and how pissed off I am that I didn't get one that I don't have to keep in the bedside table in a Taco Cabana bag. Yes, that's been difficult. But that really only bothers me when I can't have sex the way I was meant to have it. I assure you I am not having sex all the time, because I'm middle-aged, and we have HGTV. And then there are the *Little House on the Prairie* reruns that I dig because I like seeing Laura Ingalls kick Nellie Oleson's ass.

The part of my body that really bothered me was my lady chest, only I didn't realize how much because it's just my everyday loose change, right?

When I was twelve or thirteen, my mom gave me my first training bra because she said it was time for it. I wasn't very well-endowed, but my mom had rules. It was a ratty beige hand-me-down from my sister who used it when she was eight or something, because she really had some knockers. Every time I put it on, I felt stupid and humiliated and wondered what exactly this was helping me to train for. It certainly wasn't going to do anything for my softball game. I was not elated about the prospect of puberty like some of my friends, who would all giddily show each other their bras in the locker room and act like this was an exciting thing while I hid in the corner behind an open locker door and got really fast at taking my shirt on and off.

But, you know, you get used to stuff. I've seen people get used to not having an arm or having an allergy to every food they love. If you absolutely have to, if you have no choice about something, you can get used to some pretty heavy stuff and just keep moving forward.

I kept moving forward and grew up and knew my body was all wrong, but I sure as hell wasn't ready to say anything to anyone, like, "Hey. This isn't right. I hate myself. Someone help me figure this out." Nope. I just kept going. My breasts weren't very big and luckily baggy shirts were in in the '80s, so I could at least hide a little. Then sports bras showed up: big win.

That's how I lived for so long. Every time I looked at my body in the mirror, the thing I hated the most were my boobs. My father was really into bodybuilding when I was young, and his muscle magazines were all over the house. I'd take them into my room to turn the pages and stare and stare at how beautiful their male bodies were. Their chests were so nice. When I looked at myself in the mirror, even if I was in prime shape, I never once thought I looked good. Not even okay. Because my breasts were always there, looking back at me, ruining everything.

Then, as I told you, God fucked with me a little more when I turned forty-five. Imagine you are a middle-aged man. You go to bed one night and you're slightly okay with your body and everything is fine. In the morning you wake up and suddenly you have the most tremendous rack that could rival Phoebe Cates getting out of the pool in *Fast Times at Ridgemont High*. Yes, my boobs became that incredible. I know what some of you people out there are thinking: *Oh, my God, I wouldn't stop touching myself.* But this was the opposite of that.

It was horrible. My girlfriend was super excited, because Phoebe Cates's boobs were super hot; I still google that shit sometimes just to look at her. I couldn't blame my girlfriend, but I was absolutely horrified. It was like seeing the clown from *IT* looking at me from the sewer every day when I looked in the mirror. I grew even more uncomfortable. I stopped wanting my girlfriend to pay any attention to that part of my body because it felt alien to me. I started wearing a shirt during sex. I started buying smaller and smaller sports bras and even a binder to keep them down and hidden, but there was no way I could hide them anymore. My loose change got a lot louder in my pocket, and it just about covered my closet floor when I undressed, but I still kept kicking it to the corner and moving forward.

Until I realized that I didn't have to. Now, you would think that I would have jumped at the chance to make things right when Captain Gender Reassignment Surgeon showed up at my hospital to do top and bottom surgeries for trans folks. (Even though God likes to fuck with me, he occasionally tosses me a bone.) Or maybe when I started seeing all these guys roll out of the OR with their beautiful, flat masculine chests. Or perhaps when they told me that their top surgery day was the best day of their lives because suddenly these things that are seen by our society as, if not sexy, then at least overtly feminine, were gone. Or maybe when my hospital started talking about covering these procedures for their employees. Nope.

What made me realize that I didn't have to kick any more pennies was a day I'd been to the pool. I was sitting in the backyard with my girlfriend in my bathing suit, which had evolved into board shorts with a sports bra/bikini awkward hybrid thing covered by a loose swim shirt. I looked like a seven-year-old at a water park. Aside from the normal amounts of embarrassment and humiliation I have about how I look in that, like when I watch my girlfriend dance and can see that it makes everyone around her uncomfortable and want to run away, I was pissed that my boobs were still all wet and cold under this stupid getup. I complained loudly about it to my girlfriend. She responded, "You're miserable. Why don't you just get top surgery? The surgeon is, like, your BFF, for God's sake. You have the golden ticket." Just like that, I realized that I could do it, that I wanted to do it. I didn't have to live with my body the way it was anymore and suffer and kick that fucking change around and act like it didn't exist.

My girlfriend, who had loved my breasts when they were available to her, who had accepted when they weren't and had taken some time to realize the extent of my hatred of them and maybe didn't understand how big a deal this was to me for some time, was the one who set me free.

Within five minutes, I texted the surgeon and told him what I wanted to do, and his response was, "FUCK YEAH!" Then I jokingly asked him if he could make a dick from titties, and he said, "Kind of like making a diamond out of two pieces of coal! Also, no."

It takes years for people to get in to see this surgeon. That's how good he is, and that's how many miserable people there are in the world. Yet, by the grace of my circumstances, I had a surgery date scheduled by the next day. That week, I had my pre-op appointment—I ambushed him in the staff lounge at work, shamelessly lifted my scrub top, tank top, and sports bra, and said into his wide eyes, "See? They're fucking huge, bro. Get rid of them." He agreed that they were indeed huge, and within two months, he performed my surgery.

Five days after surgery I went for follow-up and could finally have my binder and my dressings removed to see my chest. You know when you have those really great moments in your life, like maybe when your children are born or when you discover that there's a search feature on your porn site where you can type in absolutely anything you want and see it? Well, this was better. My chest was finally correct, even though my freshly removed, resized, and replaced nipples looked like scabby pepperoni the size of nickels. I didn't care.

I've had several of my trans patients tell me that all of their dysphoria disappeared instantly when they woke up from surgery and looked down to see their new dicks for the first time. I certainly believed them, but I didn't understand what exactly that must have felt like for them until that Tuesday in the office. Even though they have a really shitty small handheld mirror in there (and need to get a full-length one if they want to be legit), the second I saw my chest, *all* of my dysphoria was gone. In a puff of smoke and pepperoni, the thirty-seven cents was gone, and it wasn't on the floor. It was in a trash can in the operating room.

So I lied to you in the last story when I said I wasn't going to change my body at all because I was already a butterfly. I just didn't know yet. Sometimes you don't realize the extent of what is living just beneath your surface, even when you hear it every day and even when you see it staring back at you in the mirror. Sometimes you also don't realize that perhaps you have options to make yourself correct, to stop all the hating.

That's exactly what happened to me. I very suddenly stopped hating myself. Now I don't know what to do with this amount of happiness. I feel like someone just let me out of prison and it's perfect weather out and the chirping birds are happy to see me and I just found a million dollars, and then Phoebe Cates gets out of a magical pool located next to a correctional facility, undoes her bikini top, and says, "Hi, Holly."

I have what I've always wanted, and it looks glorious!

thanks a lot, life

/ found out George Michael died during breakfast on an island
near the southern tip of Vietnam. I was eating my *bun cha* and
scrolling through Facebook when I saw it and said out loud to my
noodles, "George Michael died." As I did, I heard two people at the
breakfast table next to me say the same thing. They were Americans in their late forties or fifties. They were eating pancakes, and
I heard one say to the other, "Who is George Michael?" The other
said, "I don't know." I was immediately sad for them.

*George Michael was a beautiful, talented angel sent here by a God who
wants us to be happy* is what I wanted to tell this oblivious couple sitting next to me. But you kind of need to mind your p's and q's when
you travel to places like Vietnam, look like a dude, and are eating
breakfast in a sports bra.

Within one month of his death I had two powerful dreams
about George Michael. In the first one, we were in love. I got to
gaze upon his beautiful face while he smiled at me. I was with the
Faith era George. I kept stroking his stubbly chin and marveling
at how his gold cross earring glinted in the sunshine. He wore his
leather jacket the entire time even though it was hot outside, but in
the dream, in those tight jeans, it made total sense.

In the second dream, he came to me as a part of Wham! He and Andrew Ridgeley were young and had a beach house and we all lived together. I ignored Andrew Ridgeley the entire time because who ever cared about him anyway? Young George, with his feathered hair and tiny shorts, took me by the hand and introduced me to someone and said, "This is your spirit guide." He and George then took me to a house where they showed me all kinds of details about my life to come. My mom showed up in this dream, but she just floated past me without saying anything. I woke up and scrambled for my notebook. There was so much specific and helpful information to write down, and I was excited. But I was also confused.

My mom had passed away two years ago. When she left us, we weren't on great terms. We were never on great terms. She had been difficult and unhappy and angry the entire time I can remember, and I was tired of listening to her bitch about everything. She had survived cancer eight years before. I had hoped that might make her finally appreciate her life and perhaps enjoy whatever extra time she got. Instead, she became even more bitter, blaming everyone around her for her unhappiness. I couldn't understand it and I was over her shit and I wasn't good at hiding my feelings. When I knew she was near the end, I booked a trip to visit her even though I understood that she didn't want me to. Before I went she told me, "I don't want you to come." My response was, "You can't stop me." Such warmth from both of us. The final words she said to me as I was leaving her presence for the last time were, "As soon as you leave, your father and I can go to Walmart." That was that. I drove off in my rented Corolla and looked for a trash can to stealthily throw away my empty tequila bottle. A month later she died in her sleep after eating a Big Mac and drinking a glass of wine. Good night, Mom.

The day after she died, I was in Safeway buying beer for my dad, and I slipped and fell in a pile of cottage cheese that someone had dropped on the floor in the checkout line. As I was lying on the floor with the manager and several customers gawking over me, asking if they should call 911, I held the beer close to my chest and thought, *Well, my mom's dead, and now I'm lying on the floor in a pile of cottage cheese. Thanks a lot, life.*

I'd since been waiting for her to come and talk to me about things. Not about the cottage cheese. I wanted her to explain herself to me, to tell me why it was so hard for her to love us. Why she would lock herself in her bedroom for days when we were kids and let me slip her love poems, which she would never acknowledge, under her door. Why she could be so happy to dance and sing around the kitchen table while we ate our tomato and mayonnaise sandwiches, but then would pull us out of bed at 3 a.m. for a family meeting that ended in her threatening to pack her bags if we didn't do better, didn't try harder. How do you try harder when you're ten? I wanted to know, felt I had a right to know. I'd spent two years waiting to hear from her in a dream, or see her in a shadow, anything to help me understand what happened to her, and I got nothing.

But here was George Michael, showing up a damned month after he died to tell me he loved me *and* to introduce me to my spirit guide while my own mother floated by with a blank face and her mouth closed. What the fuck, Mom? George was nice and all, but I needed answers. This was so unfair. After that dream I became sadder than I've ever been. I woke up the next night with a heavy empty feeling that wouldn't let me sleep. It was so devastating that I called in sick to work. I never call in sick to work, but I just couldn't stuff all of that sadness into my uniform. I decided to take a drive and found myself on the road to Blanco State Park, even though it was cold out and I wasn't wearing socks.

On the way back, after sitting at a picnic table in front of the tiny falls while my ankles froze and I wrote nothing in my journal,

I listened to an audio book that I'd gotten months before. The book was *The Light Between Us*, which is about a psychic medium who talks to people who have died and helps their loved ones deal with grief and loss. I don't know how I found myself listening to this book. I don't ever listen to audio books because I generally think they're annoying. But I listened to this one and cried the entire fifty-nine miles home. I went inside and listened to it in bed and cried for another hour. And then I was all, *Duh, Holly. Why don't you find a medium to help you talk to your mom already?* I googled Laura Lynne Jackson, the author, but she is now booked out for five years. I certainly couldn't wait that long, so I looked around the Internet for another certified medium, because that's a thing. I found one in Kyle, Texas, who had great Yelp reviews, because that's also a thing. You can Yelp your medium!

I made an appointment with Elizabeth Stanfield and spent the next week waiting nervously, trying to tell myself that, you know, it was no big deal. It probably wasn't real and wouldn't change anything.

That Sunday came, then 3 p.m. came. My phone rang. It was the medium calling to give my reading. She said a prayer and asked me some brief questions about what I wanted, and we began. I'd been intentionally vague with her regarding any details of my life. I needed her to prove to me that this was real.

She started telling me about my grandparents. I didn't recognize them from her description, but the medium was certain they were my grandparents. They then told the medium my aunts' names to validate who they were. They name-dropped Georgiana and Marjorie like it was no big deal, except those are indeed my aunts' names. Apparently, my grandparents are around me all the time and sit with me on the couch when I'm sad. They told her I'm a writer surrounded by notebooks and pencils, and that I'm working on a book. They are smiling and clapping for me. They also told her that I drink too much and need to take vitamin D and B-12. Oh, okay, medium. Now I see why you're getting good Yelp reviews.

Next she said she saw a young male hanging around. She said he was handsome and was standing with his hands on his hips. "It's George Michael," she said. I swear to God that's what she said. I have the reading on MP3 if you don't believe me. It's at this point that I lost my shit and started jumping up and down in my office. "He is playing a song for you," she said. "He wants me to sing it to you. *Well I guess it would be nice / if I could touch your body . . .*" and the medium and I both sang "Faith" together into the phones that connected us. When we were done singing and laughing, George Michael had a lot to tell me. He told me through the medium that it was important to strongly be me and to believe in myself. He said that now is my time to roar, that this book needs to get out into the world because it will help people to understand things, and to tell other people to get out of my way while I do what I need to do. He said I am never alone and everything real is always about love. George Michael showed up for my medium along with my grandparents and then together they told her what the title of this book should be. I'd been struggling to make a decision between two different titles, and it was tearing me apart. The title of a book is an important thing, right? They told the medium like they'd all been reading my notebooks. Oh, God. My grandparents were reading my notebooks.

We were now going on forty minutes into my reading and she hadn't mentioned my mom yet, so I finally asked the medium about her. Almost immediately she said that my mom was here and started telling me what she was saying. There was a lot of vague information from her. I wanted to believe my mom was really there, but much of it felt irrelevant. This went on for a while until it was time to end. I thanked her profusely, and we ended the phone call.

When my reading was over, I sat trying to wrap my head around it. It was just another Sunday afternoon, except George Michael and my grandparents came by to chat, encourage me in my endeavor, and give me the title of this book. I was disappointed that I didn't get anything significant from my mom, like she had ghosted me again. Maybe this was just going to be how it was, or maybe I'd try again another time. The truth was that I had gotten so many great things that I couldn't be all that upset about it.

I went outside to tell my girlfriend about the reading. She had agreed to stay in the backyard with the dogs while I was on the phone so I wasn't disturbed. When I walked outside, after I sat and told her about the reading, this is what my girlfriend told me:

"I was out here praying for you to be able to speak to your mom. While I was praying, your mom came to me and very clearly told me to go inside because she couldn't get close to you except through me. I went into the house, and she dictated a message for you. Your mom said she was in the wrong life. You couldn't get to know her because she wasn't in the right life and she couldn't be herself in any part of her life. It made her very unhappy and unable to talk about it. You never saw it, but she was talented and had a good stage presence, but she couldn't pursue her dream of being a famous opera singer and that took all of the joy out of her life. She sees you on stage now, telling your stories, and she's so proud of you. She says you don't know it, but you got your talents and your dreams from her."

My mom didn't really show up for the medium, but she showed up for my girlfriend, who had frantically scribbled down the message for me and delivered it to me while I sat sobbing and shaking in a lawn chair under a tree. It was definitely real, and it changed everything right away.

My mother didn't pursue her dreams because she got pregnant when she was seventeen and had no choice at the time but to stay home and raise her family. She was angry because she couldn't be who she was supposed to be, and it swallowed her up. I couldn't possibly be upset with her anymore. Not only because it wasn't her fault, but also because she gave to me these dreams of being up on stage in front of people, telling my stories and writing this book. This is from her. Now it all made sense.

I called my sister shortly after this happened to tell her, hoping it might help with her feelings about my mom, but it changed nothing for her. My sister is still angry, and I get it. If I didn't have these dreams to write and perform and be something bigger than a normal life would allow, I wouldn't understand either. If I couldn't find a way to do this, grief and bitterness would swallow me up also.

My mom should have been a famous opera singer. She, George Michael, and my grandparents are hanging out and watching me, this weird little sensitive, awkward kid who was so ashamed and teased, who felt like a monster for most of my life, who gets to show up here 100 percent myself, fulfilling my dreams. By embracing myself completely, with the help of what my mother gave me, I've been granted the gift of finding exactly where I fit in this life. That's the secret, isn't it? We are put here to be ourselves, to bumble and shine like the tenderhearted fools that we all are. My mom would tell you now if she could: don't hide yourself away. Even if your ship is a little ridiculous, you'd better learn how to sail the shit out of it, because if you do, it will eventually carry you to somewhere beautiful. And if George Michael sings to you, you'd better fucking listen.

epilogue

So here we are, a little later on. I haven't heard from either
George Michael or my mother since that day I spoke with the
medium, but I've since placed their pictures all over my house to
make myself think of them often. I previously had no pictures of
my mother up. I was so angry with her that I kept them all in a box
and refused to look at them. Now I've put up several. In particular the ones where she is young and seems happy, as this is how I
want to remember her. Is it bad that I want to remember her in
her life before she had me? Sometimes I wish I could go back and
take myself away to give her herself back. I like to imagine her
as a giant, famous opera singer with throngs of adoring fans and
fancy clothes and a full passport and zero stupid kids to ruin it. I
don't have a picture of that, but I do have the happiest one of her
I could find perched on my writing desk. She is young, laughing,
and drinking beer at the lake. She's holding a plastic bat up in the
air that she's about to use on my dad's head. I bet she hit him pretty
good.

I have a shrine to George Michael out by my garden. My friends
think I'm a little nuts, but it feels right having him there, dancing in
his tight little jeans among the sunflowers. The tomato crop sucks

this year, but I blame it not on him but on the expensive dirt I chose to plant in. I should know better: the really good stuff grows out of plain old regular dirt.

I'm still the dick whisperer at work. I continuously can't believe that I've landed in the perfect place and time by complete happenstance, all dreams and luck and impulsive decisions. Was this the plan for me all along? Is the Universe so damn good that It began hatching this plan from the first time I snuck into my brother's room to try on his Batman underwear?

I was often teased in my family for flying by the seat of my pants, having no plan, being so messy and disorganized that I probably had a colony of roaches living under my bed. There were no roaches, but I did stuff my SAT application under there and didn't find it until the day before it was due. That's right: I almost didn't even take it, and I would have missed my scholarship and probably wouldn't have been able to go to college. Whoops. Career choices, places to live, houses, cars, furniture, all the same: whoops. Choosing my girlfriend was also like that. I saw her picture and thought, "She has a nice face." I invited her to a show, took a shot of tequila out of someone's cleavage, and nonchalantly asked her out. Why she said yes, I don't know, but we went out and didn't really like each other, but kept going out because we couldn't think of a reason not to. She became my biggest cheerleader and the person my mom trusted to speak to me through. And even though we never got married and ended up separating after five and a half years, I'd still call it a good run while it lasted.

Every New Year's Eve while we were together, my girlfriend sat down to go over her resolutions from the previous year to evaluate them. Then she would carefully plan out her new resolutions and painstakingly write them down in different colored markers. She would look at me and say, "Let me guess. Your resolution is the same as last year's: fly by the seat of your pants and have it all work out again."

Yup. The Universe sure seems to know what It's doing. So maybe I don't have to.

Cheers, Mom.

Photo by: Unknown

about
the author

Photo by: Lisa Hause

Holly Lorka is a writer, storyteller, and retired stand-up comedian whose work has been included in several anthologies and podcasts, including Dan Savage's *Hot Mic*. Her stories of gender, sex, and shame have earned her a following in Austin, Texas, where she lives and works as an ICU nurse and super sharp wedding officiant. *Handsome* is her first book.

SELECTED TITLES FROM SHE WRITES PRESS

She Writes Press is an independent publishing company founded to serve women writers everywhere.
Visit us at www.shewritespress.com.

You Can't Buy Love Like That: Growing Up Gay in the Sixties by Carol E. Anderson. $16.95, 978-1631523144. A young lesbian girl grows beyond fear to fearlessness as she comes of age in the '60s amid religious, social, and legal barriers.

Stutterer Interrupted: The Comedian Who Almost Didn't Happen by Nina G. $16.95, 978-1-63152-642-8. The funny, revealing, and unapologetic tale of how Nina G became, at the time she started, America's only female stuttering stand-up comedian.

Blue Apple Switchback: A Memoir by Carrie Highley. $16.95, 978-1-63152-037-2. At age forty, Carrie Highley finally decided to take on the biggest switchback of her life: upon her bicycle, and with the help of her mentor's wisdom, she shed everything she was taught to believe as a young lady growing up in the South—and made a choice to be true to herself and everyone else around her.

Once a Girl, Always a Boy: A Family Memoir of a Transgender Journey by Jo Ivester. $16.95, 978-1-63152-886-6. Thirty years ago, Jeremy Ivester's parents welcomed him into the world as what they thought was their daughter. Here, his mother—with Jeremy's help—chronicles his journey from childhood through coming out as transgender and eventually emerging as an advocate for the transgender community.

Queerspawn in Love by Kellen Kaiser. $16.95, 978-1-63152-020-4. When the daughter of a quartet of lesbians falls in love with a man serving in the Israeli Defense Forces, she is forced to examine her own values and beliefs.

Daring to Date Again: A Memoir by Ann Anderson Evans. $16.95, 978-1-63152-909-2. A hilarious, no-holds-barred memoir about a legal secretary turned professor who dives back into the dating pool headfirst after twelve years of celibacy.